Praise for **CEO Dad**

"Tom Stern manages to put the 'fun' into 'dysfunctional' in this hilarious account of his transformation from an aggressive, self-absorbed, work-obsessed smart-aleck into a kinder, somewhat gentler wiseacre—emphasis on wise. If you or a CEO Dad need help prioritizing, make this book a priority."

Ann Pleshette Murphy, parenting contributor to *Good Morning America;* author of *The 7 Stages of Motherhood*

"Tom Stern's genius is his ability to show the funny side of a very real problem afflicting America: how to succeed in business without screwing up your family. And while many of the situations he describes are breathtakingly dysfunctional, if not downright improbable, they will seem very real to the families of today's overachievers."

Charles S. Dubow, director of new products, Business Week Online

"I have always held that the world of work is endlessly ripe for satire, ridicule, and laughter. What we have lacked is someone willing to make this a full-time job—a kind of 'court jester' who delights in telling the king the truth, week in and week out. But now, at long last, we have found this person in Tom Stern, for whom yesterday's king is today's CEO Dad. Bravo, Tom! Bravo, bravo! May you live a very long life."

Dick Bolles, best-selling author, *What Color Is Your Parachute?* 2007

"CEO Dad is the Microsoft of business comic strips!"

Jim Impoco, former business editor, *New York Times* Sunday

"Relentlessly laugh-out-loud funny, Tom Stern has written a very wise book. As with all great humorists, Stern has something important to say: what is really meaningful often gets obscured by ego and avarice. Brilliantly conceived and delivered."

Greg Feldman, chairman and CEO, Wellspring Capital

CEO★DAD

CEO·DAD

How to Avoid Getting Fired by Your Family

TOM STERN

D|B

Davies-Black Publishing
Mountain View, California

Published by Davies-Black Publishing, a division of CPP, Inc., 1055 Joaquin Road, 2nd Floor, Mountain View, CA 94043; 800-624-1765.

Special discounts on bulk quantities of Davies-Black books are available to corporations, professional associations, and other organizations. For details, contact the Director of Marketing and Sales at Davies-Black Publishing: 650-691-9123; fax 650-623-9271.

Visit the Davies-Black Publishing Web site at www.daviesblack.com.

Illustrations and cover art by Max Miceli
CEO Dad family characters designed by C. Covert Darbyshire (*New Yorker* magazine)
Comic strip illustrations by Phyllis Hofberg Bruskin, C. Covert Darbyshire, and Joyce Pacheco

11 10 09 08 07   10 9 8 7 6 5 4 3 2 1
Printed in the United States of America

Library of Congress Cataloging-in-Publication Data
Stern, Tom
CEO dad : how to avoid getting fired by your family / Tom Stern. — 1st ed.
    p. cm.
ISBN 978-0-89106-225-7 (hardcover)
1. Leadership. 2. Executive ability. 3. Management. I. Title.
HD57.7.S735 2007
650.1—dc22

                                                                        2006102446

FIRST EDITION
First printing 2007

To Lisa, my wife and my teacher.
Thank you for grading me on a bell curve.

Contents

Foreword

The first time I read this book I literally could not put it down. I was also in stitches most of the time. I don't know if I've ever read anything so funny. Yet at the same time there was a continual subliminal message that came through of "things that matter most," namely, family.

A few years ago I remember studying the deathbed literature, which, by the way, is quite extensive. Its compelling message is that no one on their deathbed wishes they'd spent more time at the office, or watching television, or being involved in things of secondary importance.

Oliver Wendell Holmes once said, "I wouldn't give a fig for the simplicity on this side of complexity, but I would give my right arm for the simplicity on the far side of complexity." The core message of this book is on the far side of complexity. It is both simple and profound. It is also profoundly needed in a world that seduces us into putting second things first and first things second.

The simple, profound message of this book "takes" because of the medium of humor—laughter. Laughter is the great humanizer, the great leveler. It opens us up, softens the blows of hard learnings, and diffuses our defenses, particularly the defense of denial.

An uptight, anxious, impatient world has taught us that the key to life is *efficiency.* The reality is, because people have the power to choose, efficiency with *people* is ineffective. Efficiency with *things,* however, which have no power of choice, is effective. The efficiency attitude of many CEO Dads turns people into things. Maslow put it this way: "He that is good with a hammer tends to think everything is a nail."

In a very real sense, the essence of this book is "caught" rather than "taught." Humorous, historical, and real-life incidents and situations get you so emotionally connected that the top three takeaway points of each chapter are inductively "earned" rather than "learned."

The underlying, affirming message of this book is that, through self-awareness, we have the freedom and power to choose our response to any given circumstance. We are not victims of our circumstances—our upbringing, our genetic tendencies, even all of the CEO command-and-control modeling that surrounds us.

The challenge is "fish discover water last." They are so immersed in water that they are unaware of the reality in which they live. So, too, people are unaware of how their biological and cultural DNA impacts them. They simply think that's the way things are, until someone uses the unique human endowment of self-awareness. This is the great gift that separates us from animals and inanimate objects, that enables us to stand apart from ourselves and examine what's really happening. Self-awareness also empowers us to realize we have options. We have choices. We can think and do otherwise. We can become bilingual: efficient with things but effective with people. We can transcend the "control freak" modeling and tendencies that make up so much of our world.

Author Tom Stern is what I call a true transition figure. A transition figure is one who breaks established habits and rituals and patterns of life and begins new habits and patterns based on hard-earned insights and precious wisdom. From his own protracted, traumatic experiences, he learned the hard way what matters most.

In the death camps of Nazi Germany, Viktor Frankl became a transition figure by simply changing his question from "Why me? Why should I have to suffer so at the hands of these Nazis because I am a Jew?" to "What is life asking of me?" By standing apart and observing his own involvement and asking such a simple yet profound question, he exercised both his self-awareness and his conscience and became the father of logotherapy. His book *Man's Search for Meaning* has become a powerful change agent for millions of people around the world.

My first experience with Tom Stern was being interviewed on his radio program called *Opportunity Knocks*. It was simply the most delightful, fun, enjoyable—even insightful—media hour I have ever had. The synergy he, his partner, and I developed produced a quality of interaction and enjoyment that I will never forget, and it introduced me to this amazing book.

Interestingly, even though this book is primarily focused on replacing the CEO Dad formal authority/efficiency/control approach with a truly sincere, humane approach, the same essential message is also needed in the world of organizations outside the family setting. We are moving from an Industrial Age based on *control* to an Information/Knowledge Worker Age based on a *release*. However, even though we now live in a Knowledge Worker Age reality, most of our management practices are still mired in the control mind-set of the Industrial Age. Organizations still seek to motivate their people by "carrot and sticking"—the Great Jackass Theory of Human Motivation that entices in front with the carrot of reward and threatens behind with the stick of punishment. Even the financial accounting system calls *people* an expense and *things* an asset.

Most people have never really found their voice in their work, partly because the CEO Dad-itude has been institutionalized into the very structures, systems, and processes of the organization. However, the organizations that have broken with this formal authority/command-and-control mind-set are the ones that are producing sustainable, superior results, winning cultures, recommending customers and distinctive contributions. These are the organizations that are achieving true *greatness*.

There is so much to be learned from the basic, most important unit in society—the family. Great leadership in the family and outside the family comes from moral authority, not formal authority. Those with formal authority but not moral authority will find their influence withers—it's not sustainable.

I know you will thoroughly enjoy this book, and, hopefully, will catch both Tom Stern's message and his medium. To the four basic needs—to live, to love, to learn, and to leave a legacy—I suggest adding one more—to laugh.

—Stephen R. Covey

Acknowledgments

First and foremost, I'd like to thank my father, who showed me how to go out into the world and get things done. He's never found me overly funny but, ever the contrarian, it only made me want to be funny that much more (you know, that whole bottom-less-pit-of-seeking-approval deal). Conversely, I'd like to thank my mother and sister for laughing at everything I ever said and making me feel much more talented than I actually am. Also, I want to thank my brother for showing me that being a sensitive man can be a good thing.

I'd like to thank my wife, Lisa, and our two daughters, Alexandra and Arianna, for not holding it against me when I yelled "Get out of my office—I'm writing a book!" and for being the three most precious people in the world to me. I'd also like to thank my grandma Gladys for feeding me vanilla ice cream with Bosco and rubbing my feet while I watched New York Nicks games as a child (and to again apologize for giving her that fungal infection).

Thanks to Uncle Pete for his help at the beginning. To my friends Michael Vezo, Francis Parker, Steve Mittleman, Steve Miller, David Krygier, Billy Riback, Frank Poynton, Justin

Souter, Stephanie Novick, Betty Wolff, and Richard Avedon for their encouragement. And to my editor, Connie Kallback, for saying to the publishers of this book, "Okay, his proposal for a three-volume, 1,200-page series correlating all the facets of the human personality to corporate functions as a navigational tool for leadership development stinks, but what about this other idea?"

Thanks to all the therapists who failed to help me (because, let's face it, being neurotic makes you funnier), and to the one who did, Dr. Bruce Gregory, who not only got me to open up but exhorted me not to abandon my creativity. To Spencer Green for his witty suggestions when I started the strip. And, last but not least, to my radio talk show co-host, Jimmy Napoli, whose insights, sense of humor, and shared experience played a huge role in helping me finish this book.

Finally, I'd like to thank all the CEO Dads out there for providing me with so much material.

About the Author

Tom Stern's personal experience is the inspiration for *CEO Dad*. As a child, Stern was a wise guy and the black sheep of the family, while his father, a powerful CEO and pioneer in the cable television industry, was serious and driven. Their power struggles were terrific training for Stern's career as a stand-up comedian.

After graduating from Sarah Lawrence College in 1978, Stern spent the next ten years making people laugh. He did so first as a performer, next by developing comedy programming for HBO, and finally as president of film and television for Spotlite Enterprises, an agency for comedians.

In 1989, eager to make his mark, Stern reinvented himself and began a career as an executive recruiter. To his surprise, he achieved his greatest success in the corporate world his father had inhabited. Before he knew it, Stern was CEO of a leading search firm with clients ranging from PriceWaterhouseCoopers to Sony Studios.

He spent the next ten years raising a family and pushing himself to the limit. Everything was about winning. Eventually he realized his attitude was becoming much like his father's.

CEO Dad is the creative expression of that epiphany and Stern's daily reminder to keep a sense of humor and always remember what is truly important.

Stern lives in Los Angeles with his wife and two daughters. His Web site is www.tomsterncentral.com.

INtroduction

Thank you so much for opening this book. Whether you found it on the shelf of an upscale bookstore, in a discount bin gathering dust, or under a steaming mug of joe on your neighbor's coffee table, thank you. I appreciate it.

I'm assuming if you're reading this introduction that the title of the book caught your eye. Pretty catchy, huh? It wasn't the first one I thought of. Initially I wanted the name of the book to comment on my tendency to overanalyze everything, and at the same time pay homage to fine literature and the cinema, so I thought I might use *Rumination with a View*. On reflection that seemed too cerebral, too Woody-Allen-meets-*Architectural-Digest*, so I dropped it.

Next I considered a title that dealt with my deep-rooted feelings of shame and embarrassment, but with a positive spin: *How to Make an Omelet with Egg on Your Face*. However, when I asked for feedback from colleagues, one said it sounded like a motivational speech Martha Stewart might have given to a fellow inmate, so I abandoned it. Never ask your colleagues for feedback, that's what I say.

Okay, I thought, what about something dark, something quasi-existential that sounds more substantive? But *It's Hard to Read the Writing on the Wall When You're Banging Your Head Against It* did not reflect the theme of the book as much as my immense frustration at being unable to come up with an appropriate title.

Then, one evening as I left the family dinner table early to make yet another business call to someplace where it was already morning, my wife quipped, "Do that one more time, bucko, and you're fired." We both laughed, but the narrowing of her eyes made me see that, indeed, my job as husband and father might soon be in jeopardy. I don't know if she was grooming my replacement, but I did notice that my dog suddenly got his own bank account.

So, finally, with my wife's blessing, I came up with *CEO Dad: How to Avoid Getting Fired by Your Family* because it seemed, well, on point. After all, my intention was to recount my journey through the turbulent waters of work-life balance as someone dealing with a legacy handed down by his own CEO Dad.

Titling a book is hard because it's a decision you can't take back. It's kind of like naming a child, which is why for a short period I referred to the book as, simply, "Steve." I always start with the title and then worry about content later. Seems pretty backward, I know, but I've always inverted things. Since I was small I've had dyslexia, which made growing up terribly difficult. It drove my mother crazy that every morning in the shower I would only wash in front of my ears. I also had other problems: I was a hyperactive bed wetter with attention deficit disorder. Just what any parent would hope for, right?

INtroduction

My father, a powerful CEO, was thrilled when I was born because he longed to have a child—a chance to prove to my mom that he could be a great parent and not just a man obsessed with business. I've been told many times about how he first held me in his arms, tickled my chin, and called me his "little write-off."

So, my parents got more or less what they bargained for—as in more of a disappointment and less of just about everything else. I was sent to the finest schools but got horrendous grades. I couldn't sit still, was disruptive, and spent most of each class in the hallway. One semester when my report card sported four Fs, I tried to deflect my father's anger by pointing out that this might help my draft status. (Even though it was the height of the Vietnam debacle and the military was recruiting aggressively, I don't believe they were looking for ten-year-olds.)

That was me, always the wise guy, covering my shame with a joke. It seemed to be the only skill I had, although its value wasn't clear to me. I know my teachers didn't appreciate it. Once I was so worried about being utterly unprepared for a final exam that I hunched inside my locker to hide. When Mrs. Rayburn found me and asked what I was doing, I responded, "I'm cramming." This was a contributing factor to my fourth F.

My fellow students weren't thrilled with me, either. I was a lonely child with few companions. In fact, my only real friend was my shop teacher, Stan. He wasn't very disciplined. I'm not even sure he was a great teacher, but he had a terrific sense of humor. Owing to an earlier lathe-related accident, he had only two fingers on his right hand, and he never failed to make me laugh when he held them up to the class and talked about the five fundamentals of shop safety.

The reason I'm telling you about my difficult childhood is not to engender your pity but to illustrate how my obsession with overcoming my considerable challenges fueled my desire to overachieve later in life. Unfortunately, when I finally attained some small measure of success as an executive recruiter, it led to my greatest failure—as a father and a husband.

To be honest, I'm not writing this book just for you. I'm also writing it for me. As a businessman, I need a daily reminder to slow down, to stop and smell the ink toner. Somehow, despite my best efforts, it often seems (the key word here is *seems*) impossible to do. I've learned a lot about who I am and what makes me tick, which is why I'm sharing what's in this book with you now; yet I still let myself be dragged down by the undertow of craving the next power struggle. It's only natural. I continue to fall into the trap of sparring with some bull-headed business associate, and loving it. I console myself with old thinking, which makes such blow-ups seem not only unavoidable but fun!

Recently, the CEO of a huge corporation accused me of trying to "push his company around" during a lengthy negotiation, and I spent many sleepless nights furious with him, replaying everything in my head. *Pushing his company around! How dare he? His company's worth billions and my company only puts out quarterly reports because all we ever earn is a quarter.* It wasn't fair! He was Goliath and I was David, yet he had the nerve to accuse me of wearing lifts in my sandals.

But this has always been my problem: making everything my problem. It usually ends up being about *me* and my defensiveness about my self-worth. Not long ago, a therapist asked me if I thought I was a narcissist. I told him I'd reflect on it.

He didn't find that funny and warned me that unless I dealt with my issues, I'd be a control freak for the rest of my life. And who knows? Maybe even after death. He was probably right because if I hadn't changed, the first thing I would have done when I got to heaven, like any true CEO Dad, would have been to say to God, "Look, I'm not trying to take over, but do you have a succession plan? And, by the way, I want the corner cloud."

In conclusion (if in fact you can conclude an introduction), I don't think the final frontier is space. It's stress. Think about it: Searching for intelligent life on planets millions of light-years away is incredibly challenging, but not getting angry when someone cuts you off in traffic is impossible. Well, it *seems* (key word here again) impossible. The best we can do is keep plodding forward, and try to calm down and take stock of what's really important. In doing so, we can hold on to the hope of actually figuring it all out, or at least the portion of "it" that can be figured out.

There's one skill I mastered in my youth that I have no intention of jettisoning: applying my sense of humor. Life is hard enough, and sometimes "self-help" can make it seem even harder. It puts all the pressure on us, for the love of Mike! (Who is this Mike, by the way, and why do we reserve so much love for him? Maybe we do it for Pete's sake.) We don't need self-help. We just need help. I, for one, am pretty sure I'm going to screw up a lot more on the way to enlightenment. In the meantime, I plan to sit back and laugh at how impossible the really important stuff will always be for us normal people. My hope is that, as you read this book, you'll laugh along with me.

See, it all comes back to Stan, the shop teacher with the missing digits. He made me giggle and, in so doing, helped me learn. Life's lessons are often hard won, but the ones that stick with us are the ones we can chuckle about. You've heard the expression "learn by doing." Well, if you've cracked open this book, my guess is you've already *done* quite a few things. You've already learned by doing, and somehow it hasn't stuck. So, let's create a new expression: "learn by laughing." If you're a really good student, you may even do it all the way to the bank.

But I can't leave you there. My editor tells me I have to include a quick word about what you can expect from this book, how it's structured, and all that. Let me take a little break and work out how I'm going to do that. The truth is, as far as I'm concerned, she's just being a jerk about this. I mean, really, as if you couldn't figure it out on your own.

Note to self: Don't take a break from writing. It will only give your editor time to fire off an e-mail about how any real writer would know that there is a protocol to introducing a book, and that you are stomping all over it.

So here goes: *CEO Dad* is structured from *in*troduction to *out*roduction with eleven chapters in between as a narrative of my life—more or less. I could have called it *The History of a Recovering CEO Dad,* but then you'd know how it ends.

In the first three chapters, you'll find a scientifically accurate description of the CEO Dad-itude (I'm pretty sure it's accurate, anyway; with deadlines and everything, you know, you can't verify all the information), a short review of the long history of this closet disorder, and a brief examination of the human brain and why it allows such afflictions to incubate.

INtroduction

The next six chapters tell the tale of my step-by-step failure to overcome my CEO Dad tendencies, culminating, in Chapter 9, with my actually being fired by my family. But, stick with me, people; it has an upbeat ending.

Chapter 10 shows how I worked through my misfortune creatively, by inventing an alter ego and launching the *CEO DAD* comic strip. In Chapter 11, I bring it home with the heart-wrenching story of how this other guy and I founded an anonymous organization to help people suffering from CEO Dad syndrome.

You'll laugh, you'll cry; the book will become a part of you. Can *CEO Dad: The Broadway Musical* be far behind?

You'll find "Three Top Takeaways" as a satisfying wrap-up to every chapter. These nuggets will ensure that you are left with pearls of wisdom suitable for use in your daily life.

And, don't forget, the whole enterprise comes with my unconditional guarantee: You will not finish this book without getting the distinct impression that you have read it. Honestly, what more could you ask for?

1

Understanding the CEO Dad-itude

When You Treat Your Family Like Stocks, You Don't Get Bonds

"Never, ever, ever, ever give up." **—Winston Churchill**

"Oh, lighten up, will you, Winston? **—Mrs. Churchill**

If you look up *chief executive officer* in the dictionary, you won't find anything. But let's combine the definitions of the three individual words and see what we come up with:

Chief: One who is highest in rank or authority; a leader
Executive: A person having administrative or managerial authority in an organization

Officer: One who holds an office of authority or trust in
a corporation, government, or private institution

You may have noticed that each of these definitions has one word in common: *or.* Just kidding. The word is *authority.* Okay, now let's look up *authority.*

Authority: The right and power to command, enforce laws,
exact obedience, determine, or judge

Wow! That is a boatload of authority, isn't it? Check out those power words: *command, enforce, exact, determine, judge.* Now let's look up the definition of each of these words.

Hold on, I'm getting a phone call.

That was my editor. She said if I keep doing word definitions instead of actually writing something, she'll strangle me. This only goes to show you that the CEO Dad-itude is not gender-specific; it's not limited to dads, or even to men. Take my editor, for example. She feels the need to interfere with my creative process so that she can control how this book is written.

In turn, I (continually struggling with my own need to control things) could resort to, for example, threatening to use her real name in the book in order to strike fear in her heart and regain control. She could then call her law firm, Stretchem, Hurtem, & Riphimoff, who, unable to keep *their* control issues in check, would do their best to terrify me. This would ensure litigation that would last so long that, if indeed it were to happen, it most likely would still be going on as you read this. You know what? Don't be surprised if you're called in to testify.

However, I will forestall this chain of events by not revealing my editor's real name. As a recovering CEO Dad, I do not need to sink to the level of someone who has not attained my degree of enlightenment.

The need to control is a hallmark of the CEO Dad-itude. It is the result of years of conditioning, of growing up in an environment in which material success is rewarded and we are assured that there is only one way to get it—through relentless achievement at the expense of everything else in our lives. Even things like paying attention to other people.

Hang on, I'm getting another call.

That was my lawyer. He said if I want to go back to the dictionary definition thing, my editor doesn't have a legal leg to stand on. He broke away from attending his daughter's debut as first violinist with the Vienna Symphony to tell me that. That's right, he called me from another continent, excusing himself from a meaningful family event, just to check in about a business matter. I mean, that is one untreated CEO Dad! I might have felt a tinge of guilty respect for his actions, but with the time difference his call came in at three in the morning, and I never accept business calls after two.

In any case, now that I have my lawyer's permission, let's revisit those definitions. As we established, each of the words contained in *chief executive officer* includes in its definition some kind of authority. Remember those words used to define authority? *Command, enforce, exact, determine, judge.* That means a man or woman who has attained the highest rank in business in our society did so by being encouraged to action-verb his or her way into the top spot.

Now, imagine taking a weekend road trip with your spouse and the children. A minor disagreement arises about, say, whether everyone should stop at a roadside cafe for some food or go straight to Disney World and eat at the Pirates of the Caribbean theme restaurant. You are called on to resolve the disagreement. Just try commanding, enforcing, exacting, determining, or, best of all, judging, and see how far you get.

"Don't pull that boardroom crap with me, buster, or I'll get the next plane back and *you* can traipse around Orlando with two screaming, sticky children who need to pee every nine minutes and see how you like it!"

Hold on, there's the phone again.

My lawyer. He advised me against using the above direct quote from my wife to avoid litigation. I think I'm going to keep it in, though. It adds verisimilitude, and, frankly, I think my wife is pretty proud of having said it.

Let me just say right now that I so value having a woman like my wife in my life. She is, I see now, the best thing that ever happened to me. Our wedding day sure was special. Thinking about the day I first kissed my bride gives me a warm feeling inside. It almost ranks right up there with the day I first saw the view from my corner office. I mean, jeepers, I could see the whole city, sparkling before my eyes like some previously unattainable Shangri-la, confirming my position as someone of importance, someone who had arrived, someone who could command and enforce and judge my way into history!

I'm sorry, what was I talking about? Oh, right. My wedding day. Yeah, it was good and everything, but come on! Really, you should have seen this office!

All right, I'm still working through a few issues. I never said I was a *fully* recovered CEO Dad. But I'm willing to take a good, hard look at myself in an effort to keep you, my reader, from making the same mistakes I have made, and to share my victories as well as my defeats, and to show that our problems are really universal, and to give in to my tendency to use run-on sentences when my editor isn't here to keep me in check.

Look, "editor," I promise I won't use your real name, so let's drop this whole lawsuit thing, okay? I need your help with this book, and I'm perfectly willing to work with you as long as you see things my way.

★ ★ ★ Top Three Takeaways ★ ★ ★

1. Looking up various words in the dictionary may seem like a huge time suck, but it actually fosters much-needed skills for those with CEO Dad issues. For one thing, it slows you down. For another, it forces you to take in the nuances of any given situation. Finally, it invites you to look at things in a different way. But don't worry, this is only Chapter 1, so none of this means you actually have to change.

2. You will often be distracted by people who feel threatened by the new levels of enlightenment you are welcoming into your CEO Dad nature. They will say nasty things about you and try to undermine your authority. Knowing that they do this out of fear and insecurity will help you have sympathy for them during the workday. Of course, after work, a good bar fight can temper that pesky sympathy.

3. At all costs, do not lose your sense of humor. You can catch more flies with honey than you can with vinegar. No act of kindness is ever wasted. A spoonful of sugar helps the medicine go down.

3a. You know, there's an awful lot of truth in clichés. (See number 3, above.)

2

Recognizing the Dysfunctional Roots

History Is Full of It

"Cogito, ergo sum." **—René Descartes**

"Ooh, Latin. You think you're, like, so cool, Dad."
—René Descartes Jr.

When René Descartes said, "I think, therefore I am," he never envisioned the CEO Dad of the future interpreting that as "I think, therefore I'm right." But, that is the cornerstone of CEO Dad-itude. By now, you may have realized that you live in constant danger of succumbing to the Dad-itude, and that perhaps you have messed up several times already—misunderstanding your priorities, working too hard at the expense of your personal relationships, or insulting hotel clerks loudly enough for everyone in the lobby to overhear and think you're an important person.

However far you have strayed from balancing work and life, it's important that you not beat yourself up. See, we humans are slow to learn. The fact that you are reading this book shows that you are among the very first people in thousands of years who are willing to address their shortcomings. Yes, CEO Dad-itude has been around for a very long time. Since long before there was such a thing as a corporation, long before a single CEO walked the earth, people have been obsessed with taking control and being in charge, at the expense of everything else in their lives. As the following examples demonstrate, it has taken us this long to even begin to face up to the toxic legacy of CEO Dad-itude.

In panel one of this early cave painting, man goes on yet another hunting expedition.

Recognizing the Dysfunctional Roots

Meanwhile, in the cave, wife and family already have a plentiful supply of food
and realize caveman is going out to work to avoid being with them.

Buffalo points out to caveman that perhaps he is exhibiting antisocial avoidance behavior.

Harmony is restored. Cave divorce attorney from firm of Ugh, Thump, & Clubowski keeps small retainer.

As humankind's needs moved beyond mere survival, the desire to conquer other lands and peoples arose, bringing with it some serious control issues. Let's see how the Romans did it. Here is an excerpt from the diary of Mrs. Tiberius, wife of the second Roman emperor, A.D. 16.

TUESDAY, NOVEMBER 9. TIBEY LAUNCHED ANOTHER CAMPAIGN IN CENTRAL EUROPE TODAY. FINE FOR HIM. DOESN'T HE KNOW I HAVE EMOTIONAL NEEDS, TOO? I TRY TO GET HIM TO TALK ABOUT IT, BUT ALL HE SAYS IS "STOP HASSLING ME! I'VE HAD A LONG DAY OF PILLAGING!" OF COURSE, HE NEVER FAILS TO ADD THAT ALL HIS PILLAGING MEANS THE KIDS AND I HAVE LAMB SHANKS TO EAT AND TOGAS ON OUR BACKS.

BUT THESE DAYS I JUST WANT TO CRY OUT, "TELL ME ABOUT YOUR DAY, TIBEY! INVOLVE ME IN YOUR LIFE, BEFORE OUR FRAGILE MARRIAGE BOND DISSOLVES! MAYBE YOU DON'T THINK I WANT TO KNOW THE DETAILS. BUT FALLEN, DISEMBOWELED CENTURIONS AND FIELDS RUNNING WITH BLOOD ARE PART OF YOUR WORK, AND I WANT TO KNOW ABOUT THEM!"

OH, IF ONLY I COULD SAY THESE WORDS ALOUD INSTEAD OF JUST WRITING THEM IN THIS DIARY. PLUS, IT'S SO OBVIOUS THAT MY TIBERIUS IS SUBCONSCIOUSLY LIVING OUT THE LEGACY OF HIS IDIOTIC, OVERACHIEVING FATHER. I DON'T KNOW WHAT I'D DO IF I WERE THE SON OF AUGUSTUS, SUCCESSOR TO ROME'S **VERY FIRST** EMPEROR. NO MATTER HOW HARD HE STRIVES, MY TIBEY SIMPLY CANNOT BECOME THE **FIRST** EMPEROR ALL OVER AGAIN.

THUS DO I UNDERSTAND MY HUSBAND'S DYSFUNCTIONAL IMPRINTING, BUT I GROW WEARY OF HAVING TO SEEK OUT ROMANCE IN MY LIFE THROUGH THOSE FORBIDDEN TALES TOLD IN HARLEQUIN PARCHMENTS. AND THE KIDS ARE SUFFERING, TOO. OUR YOUNGEST LAD LEARNED HOW TO TIE THE SANDAL THONG ONTO HIS FOOT YESTERDAY.

"WHERE'S DADDY?" HE ASKED WITH A CHILD'S OPENNESS AS HE COMPLETED HIS TASK.

"DADDY WILL BE BACK SOON," I ASSURED HIM.

"WHEN SOON?" ASKED THE WIDE-EYED FOUR-YEAR-OLD.

"AS SOON AS HE'S LAID WASTE SOUTHERN EUROPE," WAS ALL I COULD SAY.

LUCRETIA, OUR ELDEST, IS IN THAT REBELLIOUS STAGE WHEN HAVING HER FATHER AROUND COULD REALLY HELP. AND NOW I AM LEFT ALONE TO COPE WITH HER ACTING OUT. SHE WANTS A TATTOO OF AN ASP ON THE SMALL OF HER BACK, AND EVERYONE WILL BE ABLE TO SEE IT BECAUSE THE YOUNG WOMEN WEAR THEIR STOLAS SO LOW THESE DAYS. I SWEAR, THE GIRL LIVES TO TICK HER MOTHER OFF. AND I FEAR I CAN DO NOTHING TO DISCOURAGE IT. WITH TIBERIUS AT WORK ALL THE TIME, THERE IS NO OPPORTUNITY FOR MOTHER AND FATHER TO PRESENT A UNIFIED FRONT.

OH, WELL, DEAR DIARY, I MUST GO. I AM OFF TO SEEK SOLACE WITH MY SISTERS AT A LIVE PERFORMANCE OF THE OPRAHTAVIUS SHOW. TODAY, HER TOPIC IS "GIRL, YOU DESERVE A DAY AT THE BATHS!" HONESTLY, SOMETIMES IT SEEMS SHE IS THE ONLY ONE WHO UNDERSTANDS. SHE IS SO MUCH BETTER THAN THAT DR. PHILISTINE.

King Arthur is the embodiment of chivalry and noble purpose. But was he really just a walking bundle of CEO Dad-itude? These notes from his psychologist indicate as much.

Patient notes, 22nd May, 1311:

Patient "A" seems lost in his delusions that someone he calls "The Lady of the Lake" pushed a sword called "Excalibur" up through the water, thus making him king. When I suggest that "A" is running away from his unrequited love for Guinevere by assigning himself a larger-than-life destiny, he pooh-poohs the idea.

Meanwhile, he also fails to see that surrounding himself with similarly driven, ambitious knights (Gallahad, Lancelot, Percival, Gawain, et al.) only closes him off further from exploring his true needs. And, it opens him up to rumors that he hangs out only with men and might be a little light in the chain mail.

"A" claims that all he needs is a little time away to sort things out, so he has decided to go adventuring in pursuit of the Holy Grail. I suggest that when he gets back, perhaps he can rest and relax, but he fires back that he and the boys want to get going on building a rather large, round table for themselves. Again, people will talk.

I will be attending a psychologists' conference in a few weeks' time, and I am considering introducing a new term to our field, inspired by my sessions with this patient: "Type A Personality." I hope the board approves.

Rarely do we see historical examples of people confronting their CEO Dad-itude head-on. While scholarly opinions differ as to the authenticity of the following, many believe it to be a secret outpouring from one of America's greatest, and most notoriously introspective, presidents. It was found scrawled on the wall of a men's room in a public house only blocks from the White House in Washington, D.C. The year was 1865.

> *I question the value of my achievements and wonder if I would have been happier splitting rails. My wife is mentally unsound, a civil war has ravaged our land, and tonight I have to see this stupid play. — A.L.*

As the growth of technology accelerates, the temptation to stingily ration our time with what is truly meaningful looms over our every move. Sometimes our outward achievements may seem very important. Sometimes they may even be big enough to change the world. Still, that doesn't mean we should neglect the small, important corners of our personal universe. Take the greeting card shown on page 17, found among the effects of one of the world's greatest spiritual leaders, Gandhi.

So take heart. Greater men and women than you and I have lived productive lives despite being complete basket cases without a clue as to what they were doing wrong. Today, tools are becoming available to help us move beyond that, into a place of living productive lives despite being complete basket cases with the vague feeling that we might be doing something wrong. Now, that's progress!

I was . . .

- ☑ Holding a hunger strike
- ☑ Working for India's independence
- ☑ Fighting discrimination
- ☑ Getting nominated for the Nobel Peace Prize again
- ☑ Working at my loom

We'll get it right next time, kiddo!
Love, Mahatma

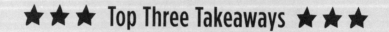

★ ★ ★ Top Three Takeaways ★ ★ ★

1. **We should take comfort in knowing that whatever problems the modern CEO Dad may have, others have had them, too.** And many of those people had to deal with them before there was indoor plumbing.

2. **Great achievements do not necessarily confer greatness as a human being on you.** Go ahead, find the cure for cancer. But if you leave a wet towel clumped up in the corner of the bathroom, you're still going down.

3. **Sooner or later, even the busiest, most preoccupied leader must face the need for warm human interaction.** Just ask Oprahtavius.

3

Stemming from the Brain

We're Out of Our Tiny Little Minds

"We fear things in proportion to our ignorance of them." **—Titus Livius**

"That's stupid." **—A kid in Titus's homeroom**

It might be useful to know what is happening inside the mind of someone like me. The brain of a person with CEO Dad-itude is as different from the normal brain as tofu is from a T-bone. Science has ignored this basic fact for hundreds of years. Why? Because the majority of scientists are overachieving work-aholics who survive on caffeine and Krispy Kremes and whose idea of family is the stuff that scurries around in a petri dish. In other words, they are dealing with their own CEO Dad-itude and don't want to delve any deeper.

In the interest of equal time, let's look at what these people have come up with. According to conventional wisdom, the brain is divided into three parts: the reptilian brain, the limbic brain, and the neocortex. The reptilian brain, they say, goes back the longest in human history, to when we were little more than slime molds desperately trying to establish a pecking order. Of course, we're still slime molds desperately trying to establish a pecking order, so this may be the biggest "duh" discovery since the recipe for ice.

The second-oldest part of the brain is the limbic brain, wherein emotions come to the fore—things like love, happiness, sadness, and hope. If these traits seem utterly useless to you, congratulations! You have CEO Dad-itude up the yin-yang and should continue reading this book. If, on the other hand, you are already fully in touch with your emotions, stop reading and start hosting your own talk show now.

The most recently evolved part of the brain is the neocortex, in which higher functions such as logic, planning, and critical judgment occur. People with undiagnosed CEO Dad-itude think they have huge neocortexes, but, at least in the case of men, it's no surprise that they would be delusional about the size of something.

In fact, my research shows that the overdeveloped neocortex of the typical CEO Dad has gone so far to the extreme with logic and planning that it cancels out all other higher functions. It's as if we've loaded our PDA with every address, phone number, lunch meeting, and passing notion we've had since the dawn of the new millennium, but we forgot to back it up on our PC. Without our data to define us, we feel like we're standing numbly in the middle of a busy intersection in our underwear, waiting for someone to point us in the right direction, and hopefully not with a certain upraised finger.

For those of us confronting our CEO Dad-itude, the toughest truth to face is that *our brains are unlike anyone else's.* The reptilian, limbic, and neocortex sections are all well and good, but they do not help the person who gets more personal satisfaction from a spreadsheet than a hug.

Fortunately, there are pioneering scientists out there analyzing the distinctive CEO Dad brain. A Swedish study by the Ha Ha, We Have Socialized Medicine and You Don't Institute recently tested a cross section of 150 CEO Dad-like subjects, who were given a battery of tests. These included such time-honored psychological profiling techniques as word association. A typical result is noted below.

Interviewer: I'm going to say some words or phrases, and you will say the first thing that pops into your mind, yes?

Subject: No.

Interviewer: I'm sorry?

Subject: Don't apologize. It's a sign of weakness in negotiations. You could blow the whole deal.

Interviewer: What deal is that?

Subject: The ten bucks I'll slip you for telling me what the right answers are.

> *Interviewer:* Look, I think we've gotten off point here.
> *Subject:* Well, go ahead, give me your little test. You won't find out anything.
> *Interviewer:* Nevertheless, let's begin. Just tell me the first thing that comes into your mind when I say, for example, "leveraged buyout."
> *Subject:* Love. Love like I've never known.
> *Interviewer:* "Your child's dance recital."
> *Subject:* Hell on earth.

The Institute also conducted group exercises designed to foster trust and teamwork among its ambitious and competitive subjects. These invariably ended in fisticuffs, or, in one case, a pie fight. Standardized tests that mixed questions about business and finance with questions about emotions and romance were revealing: 87 percent of those tested described their spouse as "underperforming."

One of the most startling conclusions of this Swedish study was the discovery that those with CEO Dad-itude devote all their main thinking to achievement and material gain. Yet, the human instinct for seeking companionship and nurturing clings on for dear life, not ready to devolve from the CEO Dad brain completely. The diagram on page 25 tells the story.

The tiny area of the brain reserved for home and family has, through years of conditioning, been squeezed out of the skull completely, resting uncomfortably in the nasal passages. Let's look at the diagram of the enlargement.

Stemming from the Brain

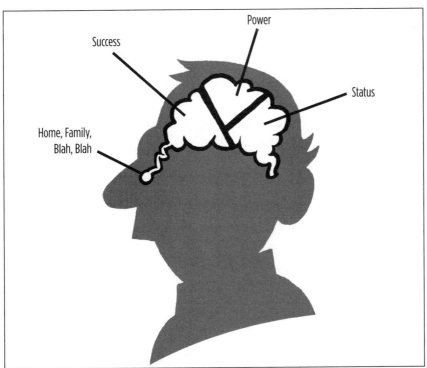

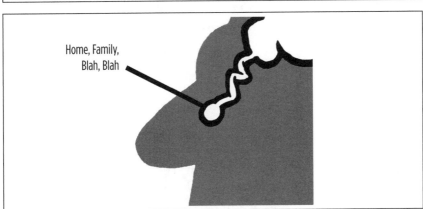

The Swedish researchers' main concerns were that the stressful lives led by CEO Dads would lead to increased colds and bouts of flu, and that the areas of the brain in charge of love and nurturing would be sneezed out of our evolution in less than a quarter of a century.

Another groundbreaking study was sponsored by the National Society of Wasting the Taxpayers' Money, in Wilkes-Barre, Pennsylvania. The researchers' conclusion was remarkably similar to that arrived at by the Swedish team; however, their costs were 30 percent higher. They, too, discovered a fourth section of the brain. Their contention, however, was that this fourth section, far from being a tiny area, is equally as big as the other sections of the brain and is locked in a continuous struggle for dominance with them. Kind of like a giant mother-in-law, but without the oversized brooch and the hat made out of plastic fruit. The researchers in Wilkes-Barre also reclassified the other sections of the brain and elaborated on their processes in an effort to reach, and possibly to heal, those with persistent CEO Dad-itude. Their findings are shown in the figure below.

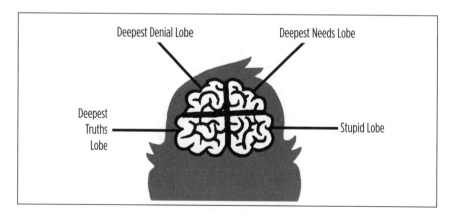

Here's how it works:

First, let's see what's going on in the Deepest Truths Lobe.

Deepest Truths Lobe
We are nothing. We come from nothing. We pale in comparison to the wonders of nature and can never equal its miracles. We're here for a short time and then we die. And, no matter what they might claim, satellite and cable end up costing you about the same.

This is truly the primal, frightening fact of our existence that stretches back to the primordial ooze. It is this that drives our unconscious feelings of inadequacy. Well, this and the Calvin Klein billboards. Confronted with our insignificance, our Deepest Denial Lobe takes over.

Deepest Denial Lobe
What do you mean, we are nothing? What about Shakespeare, Mozart, Helen of Troy, and Carrot Top? They will never be forgotten! I may never get there, but I have to try! Must get high-paying job and strive for status in the community as first step toward immortality.

Every so often, when you've worked through lunch and your blood sugar has hit the floor, for example, and suddenly everything you have to do to earn a living seems like a surreal nightmare, and you never want to see a fax machine or a telephone again, your brain's Deepest Needs Lobe rears its ugly stem.

Deepest Needs Lobe
WHY AM I WASTING MY TIME WITH SO-CALLED ACHIEVEMENT?
IT DOESN'T GET ANY BETTER THAN EXPERIENCING THE SIMPLE,
BOUNTIFUL PLEASURES OF HUMAN WARMTH AND AFFECTION.
A HAPPY HOME! A LOVING WIFE! CHILDREN . . . YES, CHILDREN
ARE THE TRUE WAY TO ACHIEVE IMMORTALITY, TO BE REMEM-
BERED! MAN, ACHIEVING INNER PEACE SURE IS SOMETHING!
YOU GET TO EXPRESS YOURSELF IN CAPITAL LETTERS! NOT TO
MENTION THE EXCLAMATION POINTS!!!!!

This is when the forces of CEO Dad-itude cry out through your Stupid Lobe, bringing you back down to earth with a simple solution to all your head-in-the-clouds reveries.

Stupid Lobe
Wait a minute. We need more stuff.

It's hard to believe this fourth section can be so stupid yet so powerful. It's kind of like a high school gym teacher who says, "Drop and give me twenty," when he can't even count that high. In advanced cases, the CEO Dad brain begins to accumulate, acquire, and achieve just for the sake of accumulating, acquiring, and achieving, until what it accumulates, acquires, and achieves is a total lack of awareness of what it has accumulated, acquired, or achieved. Which, in this case, is a tremendous capacity for redundancy. After all, if your brain insists on repeating such behavior, how will you ever know what your real needs are? The things you don't really need always seem so important. Try this simple morning affirmation as you awaken:

> *Getting by with less will bring me more.*
> (Repeat ten times.)

Wait, what am I saying? I'm talking to the CEO Dad brain, which, powered by denial and artificial stimulants, eats short phrases like the above for lunch. Here's what you really want to repeat to yourself each morning:

> On this day, do I really need an Internet hookup that is faster than my old one, and what am I going to accomplish with those extra 3.5 nanoseconds? Start a couple of Internet companies? Do I really need ninety-nine movies in my Netflix queue? I know I'll never get to *The English Patient,* no matter how much my wife says I'll love it. Is it absolutely essential that I own a car whose main new feature is a button that commands the seat to change the temperature of my rear end? Especially when I'm big enough that my rear end usually changes the temperature of my car seat?
>
> Why must these meaningless decisions become so important? Do I want AOL or Comcast? Broadband or dial-up? Version 3.0 or version 4.2? Network or cable? Do I want more protein or less fat? Chemical-free sugar or sugar-free chemicals? Should I lease or buy? If I color my hair, should I whiten my teeth? And if I whiten my teeth, can I still have my chicken blackened?

You get the idea. It's a little reverse psychology. Immerse yourself in the futility of endless striving, and you will expose the part of you that needs to slow down. Just make sure you don't expose it to anyone in law enforcement.

Now that you have identified how your brain works, it's important to start tracking what parts of your brain are operating, and when. When does the Stupid Lobe kick in during your day?

Keep an eye out for these Stupid Lobe indicators:

- You forget your anniversary. You hurriedly purchase flowers online, certain that paying extra for same-day shipping will make it all right. You are surprised when your wife force-feeds you a dozen roses for dinner and disappointed when she won't drive you to the hospital after you have trouble digesting the thorns.

- Your long-estranged parents decide to extend the olive branch and come to visit for a week. In a last-ditch effort to avoid spending quality time with them, you hurriedly institute "Take Your Parents to Work Day."

- Your child draws a crayon picture of the family, and you proudly post it on the fridge. You fail to notice that he has lovingly depicted you with a flaming head, hooks for hands, and a dollar sign where your heart should be.

Do not beat yourself up over these slips into CEO Dad-itude. The first step in correcting any aberrant behavior is to become aware of it. After all, you didn't stop belching in front of your spouse until at least the thirtieth time you were asked to.

Remember, there is good stuff going on in the other parts of your brain, too, so give them equal time. The more aware you become of your Stupid Lobe behaviors, the faster you can nip them in the bud. Devise some reminders to alert yourself to them. Put a rubber band around your wrist, for instance, and snap it every time you exhibit one of these behaviors. Watch for the times you give work and career a disproportionate priority in your life, and drop a nickel into a jar with each lapse in judgment. If you're a typical CEO Dad, don't be surprised if by the end of the week there's $4 million in there. If you're concerned about finding a large enough jar, instead have someone hit you on the head with a ball-peen hammer whenever you act like an idiot. It could work.

Most important, don't give up. That should be the easiest instruction of all because if there is one thing CEO Dad-itude fosters, it's a never-say-die mentality. As a child, did you decide not to learn to walk because it proved too difficult? Did you not learn to talk because it took too much work? Did you not learn to do laundry because someone always took care of it for you—sorry, maybe that's just me. The point is that you are genetically predisposed to succeed, so you can succeed at this work-life balance stuff, too. You *can* start tracking your reactions to life's obstacles. You *can* become more aware. This may overwhelm you at first. If it does, just go out and buy something.

I just e-mailed the first few chapters to my editor. She said the joke at the end of the chapter about buying something is too flippant and might impede my readers' learning process. I told her that I give my audience credit for having a sense of humor and that I thought it was in keeping with the "learn through laughing" philosophy I established in the introduction. She told me to blow it out my ear. Granted, she did mention that she was a little stressed out. She had just had a big argument with her husband and was calling me from Macy's, where she was using his credit card to buy herself a new wardrobe in retaliation. Honestly, I'm starting to worry about her.

★ ★ ★ Top Three Takeaways ★ ★ ★

1. **Even though the CEO Dad brain operates differently than a normal person's brain, CEO Dads should not use that as an excuse for their unevolved behavior.** Unless it allows them to close an absolutely killer deal. (Just giving you a little leeway. It is, after all, only Chapter 3.)

2. **Start becoming aware of your relentless pursuit of material goods in an effort to make up for what is lacking in your life.** "Relentless pursuit" does not include the purchase of this book.

3. **CEO Dads are programmed to succeed at anything.** Therefore, they can succeed at improving the richness of their lives. Okay, maybe *richness* is not the right word here, but you get the idea.

4

Waking Up and Smelling the Ink Toner

When All Else Fails, Blame Your Parents

"You can't build a reputation on what you intend to do." **—Henry Ford**

"Engine noise? What engine noise? Look, you want the car or not?" **—Paul Spitzer, Spitzer Pre-owned Ford Dealership, Temecula, CA**

I'll bet you thought we could all just blame our brains and call it a day. No such luck. I prefer that this book not simply supply a convenient medical excuse for being an idiot. Mostly because I've already made a deal for my second book, *A Convenient Medical Excuse for Being an Idiot.* I also need to be up-front about the fact that recognizing my problems came through hard-fought experience and a lot of pain. For example, I learned that a daughter's first steps happen only once, but the pain of a wife's knee in one's groin for missing them can haunt a person forever.

I don't know whether my CEO father missed my first steps. I do know that I've been crawling for his approval ever since. Unable to get it at an early age, I developed the fun sidelines I mentioned in my introduction: hyperactivity, ADD, and bed-wetting. Rubber sheets didn't help; they only made it easier to bounce off the walls.

I was usually in some kind of therapy as a youngster, an experience I wouldn't care to relive—hence my avoidance of introspection for the next forty years. I was not an easy patient for my childhood therapists. I drove all of them to distraction. Finally, in desperation, my parents went to extremes and hired Dr. Luigi. I can still remember him standing over me saying, "Look, kid, either you get better or I break your Legos."

That Luigi. But, I couldn't help how I was back then. I was already getting messages from my father about how to conduct myself. He spent all day forcing people to see things his way in business, and he raised me to believe that was the way to be. Trust me, you did not want to get in my way when I started pre-liminary arguments in the *Tom Stern v. Mom* battle (also known as the landmark "I demand raisin toast" case, which rocked the very foundations of breakfast). When the child psychologist gave me the square pegs test, I used a hammer to make them fit into the round holes. And it was a Fisher-Price hammer, so you can imagine the biceps I developed. At four years old, I could bench-press our Great Dane.

Waking Up and Smelling the Ink Toner

Then there were the Rorschach tests, where they hold up the inkblot and ask you what you see. Here are a few of my responses.

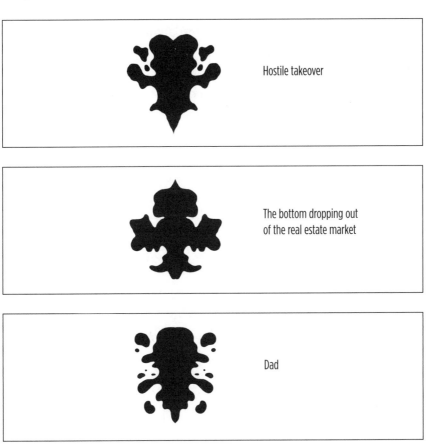

Hostile takeover

The bottom dropping out of the real estate market

Dad

After I went to college, I felt free to let my dad's expectations control me even more. For a while I resisted, spending most of my time slacking off, resenting authority, and hanging out with my circle of friend (I believe his name was Al).

But, before long, the ideas I ingested in childhood came back to me, and they seemed like the way to make things better. Soon, I was a driven, successful businessman. Imagine me as one of the nation's top executive recruiters, driving a Porsche with the top down. And it's not even a convertible. That's right, I'm so successful that I have the tops of my Porsches sawed off whenever I'm in the mood to let the wind whip through my hair! Next, imagine me at a power lunch! Then, imagine me shaking hands with a Fortune 500 business leader! Now, imagine me ignoring the needs of my wife and family as I blithely leave the dinner table early to take a conference call with that same Fortune 500 leader! Now, imagine me sleeping on the pullout sofa of that Fortune 500 leader! (Wait, how did that get in there?)

My wife and I quickly fell into adversarial roles, jockeying for positions of control in our marriage.

Good afternoon, racing fans, and welcome to the Middle-Aged Stakes. Out of the gate we've got Chloe, riding a little filly called "Resentment," pulling out in front with a zinger about how if Tom really cared, he would take more of an interest in her friends. And now it's Tom, riding "Testosterone," previous winner of the Ken-schmucky Derby, gaining the lead with that old standby about how he only works hard so his wife and kids can live in the style to which they are accustomed. They're neck and neck as they approach the home stretch . . . and . . . it's Tom by a nose, with that unimpeachable position, "You just don't understand what it's like to be me!" And Chloe returns to the stables to rest up for another contest.

Waking Up and Smelling the Ink Toner

After several years, I was so far away from taking responsibility for my actions that my wife and I were barely communicating. Whatever she said, I took it as needling. And this really bothered me because I told her again and again and again and again and again and again and again how much I hated nagging. Finally, I became passive-aggressive, retreating into a world of my work and watching sporting events.

Sports are a terrific common ground for guys in denial about their CEO Dad condition. You can spend the day ripping each other's hearts out in a complex, bitter, fight-to-the-death negotiation but end up in a bar afterward calmly talking baseball.

See, no matter how competitive men can be in business, there is always room to talk sports. After a few beers, you've got the guy in an adorable little male-bonding headlock, telling him how much you really love him. Something, by the way, you haven't said to anyone in your family since Carson hosted *The Tonight Show.* Plus, because you spent so much time in the sports bar after work, you missed dinner again. For emotionally unavailable men, that's a grand slam!

As much as I might have wished it so, it was tough to find a baseball, football, basketball, or hockey game to watch every single time I wanted to avoid confronting my emotions. I became so intent on not dealing that I would latch onto any sport just to have something to stare at while not speaking. I would watch fishing programs and pretend to find the same visceral excitement engendered by a fast-moving pro-sports contest just so people would leave me alone. "Man, have you ever seen worm placement like that?" "What a cast-off! Look at the action on the snap-back!" "And this guy's vest is remarkable . . . wow, what a lure collection!" And don't get me started on the pig races.

Eventually, it was my daughter who woke me up to how insensitive I had become. As they say, a little child shall lead them. Sometimes kids have a way of reaching you when your spouse cannot. After all, they are closer to your shins.

And they will kick. The kick in this case came from the home computer. My daughter, Grace, who is in third grade, has a blog. For anyone who doesn't know, "blog" is a derivative of "Web-log," and it's a place on the Internet where people can post anything they deem interesting about their lives. If you're like me, you wonder how these things catch on. Who would have thought there would be an audience out there for a play-by-play of a stranger's daily activities, many of them sounding like this:

> *Today I got up. I swung my feet over the side of the bed, placed them on the ground, and, eventually, stood up. I traversed the eight feet to the bathroom, where I yawned several times before opening the medicine cabinet and taking out the dental floss. You may be surprised to learn that my flossing today dislodged that piece of rutabaga I wrote about six weeks ago! Well, it's finally out. Now, if you have eleven hours, perhaps you'd like to read the next fifty-six pages I wrote about my trek from the bathroom to the kitchen. You won't want to miss the exciting description of cleaning out the gummy stuff between my toes.*

But, apparently, there's a demand for this kind of stuff. At least we don't pay for it. So, my wife was checking the parental controls on our Internet service provider (which is only fitting: the words "parental" and "control" were always left up to my wife, anyway) when she found a printout of a recent installment from Grace's blog.

> ## 11/02
>
> Sometimes my Dad is such a dorky pain. I wanted to write about how much I love my kitty-kat, and how much fun I have with my dolls, but there's no time! Dad says I have to get going on that paper for school, so now I have to collate 75 stock portfolios according to what their abbreviation on the NASDAQ is, plus I gotta follow up on the insider trading research project I'm doing, where I got those kids to give me their lunch money to invest in shadow corporations that Dad helped me invent. Whew! LTR4U! :)

I thought I had been expressing interest in my children by getting involved in their school projects. But reading what Grace had posted on the Internet gave me pause. Seeing these words in cyberspace, I was able to read them as a detached observer. I saw that Grace's dad wasn't giving her much room for anything but overachieving. And that "dorky" comment really hit home. Not to mention she got eleven postings on her comment board from her friends, all of whom agreed with her assessment of me. The next day, as I browsed through my copy of *Local Business Highlights,* a small advertisement caught my eye.

Waking Up and Smelling the Ink Toner

With shaking hands, I snipped the advertisement out of the periodical. I folded it and carried it for days, until the crease became worn and downy. As I emptied my pockets each night, I saw it among my loose change, beckoning. About a week later, after all my co-workers had left for the day, I closed the door to my office and picked up the telephone receiver. My finger trembled above the keypad. I felt a churning in my gut. I wanted to blame it on that burrito at lunch, but this was something different. Somehow, I broke through the knot in my stomach and dialed the number. I waited breathlessly through one ring. Two rings. Three rings.

I got a machine.

I hung up.

Moments later, the phone rang.

"Hello, who is this?" said the upbeat voice on the other end. The industrious little fox had *69'd me.

I said nothing.

"I can hear you breathing," said the voice. "It's always the ones who need the most help who hang up. That's why I let the machine answer. Clever, aren't I?"

Still, I did not reply.

"Suit yourself, my dysfunctional friend." Then Dr. Fine gave me his address, as if he knew I would show up at his office.

Thought he was so smart! What made him think I'd show up, just like that?

Anyway, Morton Fine turned out to be an unassuming man in his early fifties, stocky but fit, with a full head of hair extensions, tiny John Lennon glasses, and a toothy grin. After years in private practice, he had begun to notice certain common behaviors in his male patients who held stressful, well-paying jobs. He opened a research institute, intent on identifying the tendency to prize work above all else, which he called "CEO Dad syndrome." For years, he had given his subjects a battery of tests, but no one had scored high enough on them to prove his theory and legitimize CEO Dad syndrome.

Until I came along.

Truthfully, I was excited. As a CEO Dad, I was so busy using my thirst for power to make up for the lack of validation I got as a child that I hadn't stopped to realize I still wasn't getting any validation. And, now, here it was. Okay, so they were about to name a deeply troubling medical syndrome after me, but I was cool with that. It meant I was special.

It was a simple equation, really: *Daddy never told me he loved me* divided by the square root of *I'm an extraordinary mess* equals *You're really something, big guy!*

I was pumped. After all, I had spent twenty years in corporate America, where the surest way to fix any problem is to bring in a consultant. Now I was the company, and Dr. Fine was the fixer. He was going to walk into my inner corporation, set up his laptop, project a PowerPoint presentation through a big-screen TV, and show me how to achieve a greater return on my investment in myself.

Yes! I'm ready! I'll pay the exorbitant consulting fee! Just make me run more efficiently!

But then, the doubt.

Sure, I can handle anything at work. I thrive on problems on the job. Set 'em up, and knock 'em down. But this was trying to figure out how to be a better man at *home*. I have a résumé that's five pages long, and nowhere on it will you find experience in *that*.

★ ★ ★ Top Three Takeaways ★ ★ ★

1. **After a lifetime of self-reliance, it can be scary and nerve-racking to let someone else guide you to a solution.** For us CEO Dads, staring down our inadequacies can be difficult, especially since until recently we didn't think we had any.

2. **Zoning out on sports may seem like a good way to assert boundaries at home and take some time for yourself.** However, it is not, you bonehead.

3. **Paying more attention to your kids and how they respond to the lessons you are handing down will eventually mean one thing:** You're busted.

5

Being Poked and Prodded

I'm Institutionalized and I'm Loving It

> "I do not feel obliged to believe that the same God who has endowed us with sense, reason, and intellect has intended us to forgo their use."
> **—Galileo, early 17th century**

> "Please pull forward." **—Fast-food drive-thru attendant, early 21st century**

I should clarify that I wasn't completely institutionalized, not in the strictest sense of the word. I was subjected to rigorous mental poking and prodding, but I never did a sleepover. The Morton Fine Institute for the Advancement of the Curbing of CEO Dad Syndrome (MFIACCDS, not the most memorable acronym) was strictly a 9-to-5 operation. Dr. Fine saw this as fitting, since his patients, most of whom thought leaving the office at exactly five was one notch below pagan animal sacrifice, needed a reminder that the workday can eventually end.

I was glad this was not an inpatient hospital. It would have been too much to lie awake at night listening to the pitiful, demented howling of those under observation for CEO Dad syndrome. I can only imagine what their anguished wails would sound like.

I picture Phil, a Fortune 500 power player, screaming on his gurney after lights out, "Damn you! Undo these straps and let me take that meeting!"

Or Jack, former CFO of a technology giant, struggling against a straitjacket and muttering to himself, "I'll get lunch! No, no, I insist! You got it last time!"

Or Kevin, a one-time high-maintenance corporate lawyer, pacing the halls with his robe half open and talking into a banana: "I'm going into a tunnel. If I lose you, I'll call you right back!"

The fact is, Dr. Fine's facility was a small, unassuming office space in a location I am sworn not to disclose. A cozy, potted plant-laden reception area opened onto three modestly furnished examination rooms—no different from the sofa-and-chair arrangement of an average therapist's office, except for the pallet of Kleenex stashed in a corner. All they needed was a golden arch and a slogan like "100 Million Noses Blown."

In the waiting room, I formed an instant psychic bond with others who were struggling with their inner CEO Dad. Many were celebrities, so I really should not betray anonymity. For discussion purposes, let's say one of them was named "Rupert Murdoch." I found Rupert weeping into a copy of *TV Guide,* saying that if he had to wipe his nose, he'd rather it be on a publication he owned.

Another, whom we'll call "Martha Stewart," was refusing to fill out the required forms and kept trying to sell the receptionist some potpourri.

It was daunting, but also inspiring, to see that famous, notable people were as screwed up as I was. Of course, I did not yet understand that there was much of anything wrong with me.

My intake was handled by Dr. Fine's receptionist, Fiona. She was an attractive and warm young woman whose face was formed into a seemingly permanent noncommittal grin—the kind that can only come from constantly placating egomaniacs who mistake it for adoration instead of the utter contempt it represents.

Through my work with Dr. Fine and his research, I have been encouraged to share with you, my reader, every aspect of what made me the definitive test subject, CEO Dad patient zero, if you will. To that end, I have handed over all documentation uncovered by Dr. Fine in its unexpurgated form. Below, for example, is the intake questionnaire I filled out during my first visit, with my answers verbatim.

It's painful now to see how I responded, but I relive the pain so that you won't have to. Unless you're into pain, in which case you may prefer my competitor's business-themed book, *Stocks and Bondage: No Pain, No Capital Gain* by Scott "Spanky" Fisher.

MFIACCDS Patient Intake Form

Name: Thomas A. Stern

Address: 5141 Success Lane, part of the exclusive new community over near the bluffs, the house next to basketball legend Kareem Abdul-Jabbar. Really. How do you like me now?

Phone: I'll call you.

Date of birth: None of your business.

Emergency contact: Don't bother anybody. I'm fine. I can take care of myself.

Allergies: Cat dander, homeless people.

Any family history of: Hypertension? Eating disorders? Mental illness?
All three! That's good, right? Natural by-products of achieving what you want and all that. That's what I was told, anyway.

Being Poked and Prodded

1. **Rate your response to the following statements on a scale of 1 to 10 (1 = strongly disagree; 10 = completely agree).**

   "There's nothing like a new car."

   10

   "It's okay to lie in a business negotiation as long as long-term goals are met."

   Duh.

   "I wish my children would see things my way."

   Can I put "11"?

   "My spouse is happy with our income, and that's the most important thing."

   What do you mean "our" income?

   "More than anything, I could use a relaxing vacation, perhaps just staring meditatively out at the ocean each day."

   You people are sick.

2. **Recall three happy times with your father.**

   (A) Bedtime stories: Jack and the Pennystock.
   Hansel and Gretel & Deloitte & Touche.
   Goldilocks and the Three Bear Markets.

   (B) The day he told me that recess can be a valuable networking opportunity.

   (C) When he taught me how to renovate my sand castles and flip them to unsuspecting toddlers at twice the price.

3. Describe your relationship with your father.

My father was a powerful CEO and a very bottom-line kind of guy. As far as business went, he was old school. Knowing this, my mother never served us macaroni & cheese for dinner, because any kind of perceived merger would cause him to fly into a rage.

As I became more of an underachieving disappointment to Pop, my biggest fear was that on Christmas morning he would call me into his office and say, "Son, I love you very much, but we're going to have to let you go. It just isn't a good fit. Take a couple of weeks to get your toys together, and rest assured I'll give you an excellent reference if another family wishes to acquire you at some point in the future."

A visionary when it came to parenting, my dad outsourced my upbringing to independent consultants. A man named "John" was in charge of empathy, "Bob" was in charge of listening, and "Pete" was in charge of being present in my life.

Pete would appear at my birthday parties in place of my father, which was nice because he would get my name and age right. He would also stand in during parent-teacher conferences and father-son picnics. You haven't lived until you've won the three-legged race with an employee! Since my biological dad had never been seen with me outside the home, everyone assumed Pete was my father. Because there was no family resemblance, I used to tell everyone he was adopted. Pete was everything I could have wanted in a father. I loved him, but, ultimately, as is the case in life, I had to surpass him. These days, he still has a cheery hello for me as he bags my groceries. (My father had to make cutbacks in the eighties. Oh, well, that's business.)

4. What was the most valuable lesson you learned as a child?

One time, my real father showed up at my birthday party. I was turning five, and he had hired a clown for the entertainment. While I laughed at the clown's antics and balloon-animal making, my father whispered n my ear, "It may look like fun, son, but he's a grossly underpaid independent contractor." It was the best birthday present ever—learning that no matter how much joy someone like that might bring to the world, he's still just an arrested adolescent in floppy shoes with no health insurance.

5. In one sentence, describe the message imparted to you by:

Your mother: We'll take care of you financially, Tom, but emotionally you're on your own.

Your father: Ask your mother.

6. Did you have many friends as a child? What are your memories of them?

I am grateful to my father for having one of his people pre-screen my friends. My peers were required to prepare a résumé, listing their "work history" as a friend to other kids before me, how long they had lasted in those previous positions, and the reason for their termination (eraser-clapping incident, would not share the Twinkie, dissected a frog with his teeth, etc.). Then they would be interviewed, with questions such as "It says here that you are loyal, but I notice on your résumé that you ratted on Ricky Donahue when he put rubber cement in the toilet," and the ever-popular "Tell me why you're passionate about being Tom's friend." (Typical answers: "His views on the obsolete nature of passbook savings accounts," "The conductors on his train set are nonunion," and "His sister is cute." That last one put a lot of guys out of the running.) If an interview was successful, the last step would be clarifying the terms of the offer, which were usually that their friendship with me was on a six-week trial basis, and that any lunch money loaned must be refunded to Tom with 5.75% interest by the close of the next business day. All in all, it worked out well. Turnover was high, but efficiency never suffered.

7. **Which word or phrase below best describes your parents' attitude toward you during your childhood?**

    A   Nurturing
    B   Loving
    C   Warm
    (D) Dependent on end-of-fiscal-year projections

8. **Imagine yourself as a child, getting yet-another lecture from your parents on the value of a dollar. Do you:**

    A   Tune out
    B   Listen but not really absorb the information
    C   Listen attentively
    (D) Listen attentively while figuring out a way to shake them down for candy money

9. Now you are an adult, and you have just taken over at a new company. What is your first act as CEO?

   A Conduct a building-wide inspection to ensure worker safety
   B Reinvigorate employees' pension and health care plans
   C Withdraw employees' pension and health care plans
   (D) Withdraw employees' pension and health care plans, momentarily regret it, then give yourself a raise

10. An employee comes to you with a concern or complaint. You:

   A Take the time to listen to the person's genuine concerns
   B Laugh
   C Laugh uproariously
   (D) All of the above, and in that order

11. In the middle of a huge merger negotiation, you find yourself overcome with emotion as you watch your child sleeping. You:

   A Allow a calm feeling to wash over you as you think about what is really important in life
   B Feel emotional, but have a seizure as a result
   C Have a seizure just on general principles
   (D) Wake up the kid

12. Using the figures below, indicate which nautical direction the bow of your company yacht is facing:

East, Nor' East
Due North
West

Due West
Longitudinal South
North East

Due East
Due South
South South East

I'm bored. Isn't this what you pay the guy with the deck shoes for?

13. Your wife asks if the breeze through the car window is bothering you. Do you:

    A Realize she is subtly telling you that it is bothering her

    B Realize she is subtly telling you that it is bothering her, and roll up the window

    C Realize she is subtly telling you that it is bothering her, and do nothing

    (D) Realize she is subtly telling you that it is bothering her, do nothing, and mentally prepare to sleep on the couch tonight

14. Spot the incongruity in the following sentence:

    The busy CEO was too wrapped up in some important negotiations to attend his child's school play, but he made up for it by buying the child an X-Box.

    ANSWER: *A CEO should not allow his child to pursue an acting career.*

15. Which of these is an appropriate reaction to your children's failure to keep up their grades?

    A Urge them to do better next time

    B Arrange for a tutor in their problem subject

    C Withhold all love and affection until their performance improves

    (D) Arrange for a tutor to withhold all love and affection until their performance improves

16. **MATH PROBLEM:**

    On a business trip, you take a train from Chicago to Duluth, which goes 48 miles per hour and makes eleven stops. A CEO from a rival company travels from Chicago to Duluth on a plane that goes 109 miles per hour and makes no stops, but then he loses an hour and a half to parking, check-in, and security procedures. Which of you will make your board meeting first?

    ANSWER: *Two different board meetings in freaking Duluth? What are the odds?*

17. Your wife points out that you seem to have been playing favorites among your children. You immediately:

    A Tell the children you've slighted that you are sorry

    B Take pains not to encourage competition among the children for your approval

    C Find something nice to say about all the kids

    (D) See how the so-called favorite does in the dog-eat-dog world of mutual fund trading

18. In business, as in life, which definition best describes the word *uncompromising?*

    A Having a singularity of vision that inspires all

    B Charting a bold new course that inspires all

    C Pushing through to a greatness that inspires all

    (D) What I say goes

Being Poked and Prodded

When Dr. Fine got a look at my intake exam results, he was fairly enthusiastic. I believe the exact phrase he used was "EUREKA!" Plus, he grabbed me by my forearms and danced me around in a circle while singing "If I Were a Rich Man." The balloons and confetti dropping down from the ceiling were a surprise, but Dr. Fine told me he had rigged it that way months before, praying for the day someone like me would come along. The brass band seemed a bit excessive, as did Fiona popping out of a cake. But, in the end, the celebration was for me. Not only was I about to find out how profoundly dysfunctional I was, but I was going to make medical history in the bargain.

Looking back on my intake form, I can see that I did not immediately grasp what was unusual about the data I was handing over. I was just living my life according to programming that had been in place since before I could even remember. I was simply going along, and, for all I knew, I was happy. But something had driven me to start scratching at the surface. And I was stunned. When I began to scratch at the surface to acquaint myself with the depth of my personality, what did I find? More surface.

One thing was for sure: Whatever I was about to uncover, it had been there all along, waiting for me to finally get in step with it. Somebody help me. I'm starting to sound like Wayne Dyer.

Overall, what strikes me most about how I filled out that intake form is that I had no concept of my formative years being anything out of the ordinary. To this day, if pressed, I will say that the ways I was taught as a child have merit. And I certainly hold nothing against my parents.

There, that should satisfy my father's lawyers. Happy now, Pop?

Well, I've been waiting a few weeks for approval on the last couple of chapters. I finally heard from my editor. She hasn't gotten to the new material yet. She's been on a bender. I'm not sure what country she is in; the three minutes left on her calling card ran out before she could tell me. I'm pretty sure I heard a mariachi band in the background, but it could have been klezmer music. The two can sound remarkably similar, especially through a tinny telephone earpiece.

The upshot of the phone call is that I'm on my own for a while. I guess her husband found out about all the unauthorized credit card charges and told her not to come home until she is ready to apologize. Judging from the hooting and hollering that punctuated most of her sentences while she talked to me, that might be a while.

★ ★ ★ Top Three Takeaways ★ ★ ★

1. **The first step in any personal growth effort is being willing to change.** Anyone who thinks putting on a new pair of underwear is a witty response to this should be publicly humiliated.

2. **We (the untreated) are all subconsciously running our lives based on old childhood paradigms that only hold us back in adulthood.** Nothing much to add to that. Kind of sucks, doesn't it?

3. **Human beings are slow to learn.** But, when their mistakes are pointed out by someone who truly cares about their spiritual growth, they are even slower.

6

Experiencing the Great Shrinkage

The Men in the White Coats Arrive

"I love Mickey Mouse more than any woman I have ever known." **—Walt Disney**

"If you love me so much, how come you gave me only three fingers?" **—Mickey Mouse**

It's a strange feeling, knowing you are about to be put under the microscope like some lab rat. Not that lab rats get put under microscopes; they're more the run-through-the-maze or get-injected-with-chemicals type. It's really single-celled organisms that get put under the microscope. I guess I mixed my metaphors with that opening sentence, but you know what I mean.

(While she can be difficult, I do miss my editor at times like this.)

Dr. Morton Fine was over the moon. In me he had found the mother lode of work-life imbalance, and he was going to put himself on the medical map by finding out what made me tick. And, man, I was a ticking time bomb. Like an old watch, I was tightly wound. I had an internal alarm that was constantly set to "now." I'd give you a few more clock metaphors, but I'm pressed for time.

So, Dr. Fine decided that I should have a session with him three times a week. This brought on my first anxiety attack: How was I supposed to take that much time off from work? Especially to see to *my emotional needs.* It was like asking Genghis Khan to allow the Mongol hordes a sick day.

I began to break into a cold sweat on the job. Could my employees see that I was becoming softer? Did they know that I was seeking professional help, revealing my inner jellyfish? My excuses to leave for my sessions with Dr. Fine became more and more elaborate and achievement centered, to throw co-workers off the track. Like the one about the ultimate power lunch:

"Hold my calls. I'm having lunch with reps from the top three oil-producing nations, Sumner Redstone, and Bill Gates."

"Wow, really? What are you guys doing?"

"Probably getting takeout. Then buying North Dakota."

Or the one where I'm so busy, I don't even have time to open my own doors:

"Gotta go. I'm having the house wired to respond to my voice commands, and they said to meet them at home between noon and five."

Or, when I was really desperate:

"Be back soon. I'm having an affair with a supermodel!"

I wasn't, of course, but a CEO Dad would rather admit to adultery than to seeing a shrink.

Somehow, I sucked it up and made my scheduled visits to Dr. Fine. In one of our early sessions, he demanded that I hand over my PDA so he could see how I structured a typical day. In the interest of full disclosure, I include here, transcribed from its electronic format, a representative sample of my schedule.

Wednesday, March 9

6:00–6:02 a.m.	Awaken, glance at wife, consider lifting her sleeping mask.
6:02–6:40 a.m.	Brush teeth. (Dr. Fine immediately pointed to 38 minutes of teeth brushing as an example of my obsessive personality. I told him I do my best thinking while foaming at the mouth.)
6:41–7:00 a.m.	Coffee, toast, *Wall Street Journal*. (I like those stipple portraits in the *Journal*. You know, those drawings of the guys at the top of all the columns? Where they all look like they just had a prostate exam? I wonder how much those guys make?)
7:00–7:05 a.m.	Chloe upstairs waking the kids. Listen for their feet padding along the upstairs hall. Leave the house quickly.
7:06–8:55 a.m.	Commute. Skip annoying NPR, pop in Books-on-Tape of Hemingway short stories. (Angry, dissolute he-men and their long-suffering nurse mistresses in a wartime setting. Good alpha dog prep!)

8:56–9:55 a.m.	Make morning calls and kick everyone's butt virtually.
9:56–10:25 a.m.	After completing calls to family, start in on business contacts. Kick their butts next.
10:26–11:05 a.m.	If business contacts run out, call health care providers, auto leasing company, utilities, and mail order catalog operators and kick their butts, too, just for the heck of it.
11:06–11:10 a.m.	Mentally review main points needed to win last night's argument with Chloe.
11:10–11:12 a.m.	Call Chloe. Win.
11:12–11:20 a.m.	Call Client A, make final offer. It's five million, plus 2 percent on the back end, or I walk.
11:20–11:35 a.m.	Call Client B, tell him Client A is trying to make a fool of him and referred to Client B as a worthless sack of cells.
11:35–11:50 a.m.	Call Client A, tell him Client B has outbid him, even though he hasn't.
11:50 a.m.–12:13 p.m.	Call Client B, tell him Client A is willing to forgo the helipad and take just the executive washroom privileges. Unless Client B can match that, he's out. Remember to mention Client A's comment that Client B should have his brain sucked out through a straw.
12:13–12:25 p.m.	Call Client A, say deal is closed, Client B outbid him. Wait for Client A to beg.
12:25–12:26 p.m.	Take a deep breath. Realize I no longer remember who's offering what to whom or what I have set in motion.

12:26–12:26:30 p.m.	Isn't that great?
12:26:33–12:28 p.m.	Call doctor, renew prescription for antidepressants.
12:28:01–12:34 p.m.	Call Client B, give him ultimatum.
12:34–12:42 p.m.	Call Client A, say Client B backed down, even though he hasn't.
12:42–12:50 p.m.	Call Client A, accept his offer.
12:50–1:04 p.m.	Call Client B, respectfully decline his offer. Say that Client A has only the kindest words for him now that he has lost like the girly-man he is.
1:04–2:40 p.m.	Meet Client B for lunch. Smooth everything over. Get Client B to pick up the tab.
2:40–2:45 p.m.	Call Chloe. Remind her who won the argument.
2:45–4:45 p.m.	Conduct four scheduled employee reviews. Listen to Hemingway for prep!
4:45–5:00 p.m.	Avoid eye contact with four fired employees.
5:00–8:00 p.m.	Remain at work. Why? Not sure. Reason to follow. Will think of something.
8:00–9:00 p.m.	Stop off at bar for drink, snacks.
9:25–9:28 p.m.	Greet Chloe. Say I ate already.
9:29–9:30 p.m.	Walk by kids' door. Listen. If no sound detected, proceed.
9:31–9:33 p.m.	If sound is heard, open door, get sound to stop, close door, proceed.
9:34–11:00 p.m.	Sit and read new articles on old topics. Anything to avoid interacting with family.

11:01–11:08 p.m.	Check scores on ESPN. Hear Chloe puttering in next room. Say daily meditation prayer that she will not start a conversation.
11:12–11:22 p.m.	Get in pre-sleep argument with Chloe. Let her win.
11:23 p.m.–5:59 a.m.	Stew. Should never have let her win that argument.
6:00–6:02 a.m.	Awaken, glance at wife, give sleeping mask a snap.
6:02–6:02:30 a.m.	Claim not to know what passive-aggressive means.
6:02:30–6:40 a.m.	Brush teeth, 30 seconds less than usual.

I can still remember Dr. Fine's reaction to my PDA. After reviewing it in silence for a few minutes, he looked up, took a deep, nasal breath, and said, "May I borrow this? I'd like to show it to some of my colleagues."

Though I did not tell him, I was flattered. The last time anyone had asked to keep something I wrote was the day my wife saved a Post-it I had left her with the words "We'll get away next weekend, I promise" on it. She still brings it out every once in a while, along with the Post-it she left me in reply: "But, honey, I just saw the news, and there was no mention of Hell freezing over."

I was also filled with the terror of a greedy, possessive CEO Dad who was being asked to surrender one of his toys. The only way I could cover my anxiety was to adopt the tone of a man so accustomed to material abundance that the donating of a PDA was but a trifle.

"Borrow it? You can keep it! What's one PDA to me, anyway? Why, I was just heading out to buy five more on my lunch break. Yessiree, I can afford as many PDAs as I want! In fact, I have more than I need. After we're finished here, I'm going to head down to the soup kitchen and hand out PDAs to the underprivileged! After all, effective daily planning is more important than proper nutrition!

"Do you see what you're doing, Tom?" asked Dr. Fine.

"What do you mean?" I queried.

"You're overcompensating. You are nervous about baring your soul to me, and perhaps do not wish me to have your PDA, but you cover your worry with meaningless drivel about your privileged station in life."

"Oh," I said. "So then you don't really need to borrow my PDA?"

"No, I do," he said. "Psych!"

It wasn't fair. I thought I was the master manipulator of human minds. But up to now I had been dealing with laypeople, business associates, and my family, whom I could bend to my will simply by alienating them to the point of giving up on me. Now, here was an expert in the workings of the human mind, who had clearly decided he was going to make a difference in my life and not give up on me no matter how reprehensibly I behaved. And, for that kindness, I will never forgive him.

Little did I know what I was getting myself into. The "friends" to whom Dr. Fine wished to show my PDA (or "Exhibit A" as it came to be known) were none other than Drs. Winnick, Warwick, and Wise of the prestigious Middle Class White Guys with Personality Disorders Clinic, in Bethesda, Maryland.

Soon, I was under full observation, my every movement noted by three clipboard-clasping gentlemen in lab coats.

It began on the drive to work. Wise was in the front seat, Winnick and Warwick in the back. If I reached to change the radio station, Winnick would call out, "Aha!" and make a note.

If I checked my hair in the rearview mirror, Wise would comment, "I see!" and jot something down.

If I turned on the air conditioning, Warwick would say, "Hmmm," and scribble.

I felt like I was in a fishbowl, except I wasn't swimming and there wasn't any water. (Boy, that was a lousy metaphor. Honestly, when is my editor getting out of rehab?)

On day three, another motorist merged into my lane without signaling and I couldn't slow down in time to avoid him. Our bumpers scraped. The words I used in reaction to this were the same ones I would have used on any other occasion involving a careless driver. Yet, this time my profanity was being recorded by three of the nation's leading scientific researchers. A proud moment for me. Even prouder when I tapped Winnick's clipboard and said, "I believe 'dumb-ass' is hyphenated."

I got out of my car and read that other driver the riot act. As we exchanged license numbers, I proclaimed loudly how, thanks to him, I was going to be late for a crucial presentation on strategizing for maximization of minimum potential effectiveness training, and how I planned to sue him for the hundreds of thousands of dollars I would lose as a result; and, of course, I threw in additional expletives to punctuate what I thought of his dull-witted vehicle maneuvering.

And then the other driver said something that rattled me to the core. He pointed behind me and asked, "Who the hell are those guys?"

He was staring at Winnick, Warwick, and Wise with their pens at the ready. I had grown so accustomed to their presence that I had stopped adjusting my behavior to appear in the best light. Damn them!

The other driver then sighed, apologized profusely, and said his mind was elsewhere as his father had died, the funeral was tomorrow, and his oldest child had just dropped out of college to join a citizens' militia group in Montana. He looked so sad standing there at the accident scene, his shoulders drooping; I told him that we should just forget the whole thing, and we both drove off with a sense of calm and renewed faith in human nature.

This stranger made me see that I was overreacting, that I had to learn to keep things in perspective, that I needed to slow down and understand what is really important. I was so moved that I almost decided not to check out the guy's story.

When we arrived at the office, I put Winnick, Warwick, and Wise to work. If they were going to hang around me all day, the least they could do was be productive. I had them check funeral notices from the past several days to see if the last name on the man's driver's license showed up in the papers. It didn't. So, that little skunk had appealed to my sympathy with a sob story about his family woes just to avoid a costly insurance settlement. Here I was, trying to get my work and family life into balance, and I got duped by someone who was making a mockery of that goal. Of course, there is a chance that he wasn't lying, that perhaps the funeral he mentioned simply wasn't listed. Either way, I was fully committed to hating him for at least the rest of the fiscal year.

Winnick, Warwick, and Wise filled up six or seven notepads each that day. And when word got back to Dr. Fine, he said that I had made a little progress in deciding not to prosecute the other motorist, but that trying to find out if he was lying showed my control issues kicking in, striving to rearrange the outcome of events to fit my skewed worldview. It's like someone once said, "When you lose, don't lose the lesson." I hate that expression. It seems like it's geared toward losers.

Getting the staff at my office to grow accustomed to Winnick, Warwick, and Wise was difficult. To begin with, the three of them were always making free copies. That kind of thing adds up. Plus, it was awkward having to say, "Don't mind them," while discussing market trends with Bob at the urinals.

A week or so into my days as a test subject, Winnick, Warwick, and Wise came along to my tennis lesson. Luckily, they had all signed releases prior to our work together, indemnifying me should they suffer any bodily harm while observing my actions. I believe it was Warwick who ended up with the injured esophagus. All I did was throw the racket in frustration after I failed to return my snotty little hotshot instructor's well-placed ace serve. What are the odds that a tennis racket could sail halfway across a gymnasium and hit Warwick in the throat? Especially since I was aiming for his knee.

The culmination of the three scientists' involvement in my life came when they had dinner at our home with my wife, Chloe, our two children, Grace and J. D., and me. I had assumed that my family's having to adjust to these strangers in their midst would make for a stiff and reserved evening. However, I had not counted on the fact that, for the first time ever, a neutral observer was taking part in a Stern family event. They were buffers, if you will, a luxury my wife and children had never been afforded. As a result, the floodgates opened and subconscious thoughts came through unbidden during the course of normal conversation.

What follows are snippets of conversation from that evening as reported by Winnick, Warwick, and Wise. I don't remember hearing any of this, but Dr. Fine says great trauma often causes blackouts. No wonder Chloe never bought my "I was abducted by aliens" theory.

"This is delicious stew, Mrs. Stern."

"Why, thank you, Dr. Wise. My husband doesn't think much of it. He tends to internalize conflict rather than address emotional difficulties. It's long-ingrained behavior that he gets from his father. Who also hates my stew."

"Yes, I would like some more stew, thank you."

"Wow, so you guys are scientists, Dr. Warwick?"

"That's right, J. D. Got any science-type questions you'd like to run by us?"

"Um, yeah. What are black holes, and is it possible that my ADD is caused by a nagging sense of loss brought on by wishing my father were more present in my life?"

"To answer your question, J. D., a black hole is a form of space matter that sucks everything in its atmosphere into it."

"Cool. Can it do that to my father?"

....

"Did you make these cookies, Grace? They're delicious."

"Yes, thank you, Dr. Winnick. My mom helped me mix the flour and water, but I did all the rest because I'm pathologically predisposed to overachieving, having decided that it might be the way to win my father's approval."

Good job on the cookies, young lady."

"Are you saying that just because you think I need your approval?"

....

That evening, Dr. Fine's grant money for this phase of the project ran out. This was to be the last day I would have Winnick, Warwick, and Wise underfoot. I bade them a fond farewell. They were an integral part of my growth process, and I would miss them dearly.

Not.

The next day, I found a rumpled note on the floor in the backseat of my car, written by Winnick, Warwick, or Wise. It read:

"Maybe Subject Stern was right when he said that working in this low-paying, nonprofit research stuff can be a drag. He made quite a convincing argument today for getting our butts out of this government-funded ghetto and moving into the private sector."

Honestly, I don't know how I'm supposed to get better if the old stuff keeps working.

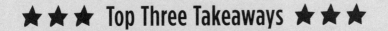

★ ★ ★ Top Three Takeaways ★ ★ ★

1. **The way you choose to organize your day is a good initial indicator of what your priorities are.** And may reveal that you are a schmuck.

2. **Trying to control the outcome of every single situation is a foolhardy endeavor and tantamount to playing God.** Then again, you could pick a worse role model.

3. **People with forceful, overbearing personalities often forfeit the opportunity to better understand the emotional lives of those around them.** And no, that's not a good thing, wiseacre.

7

Failing at Success

Somebody Down Here Hates Me

> "Men have become the tools of their tools."
> **—Henry David Thoreau, 1850**

> "I would kill for a roof."
> **—Henry David Thoreau, 1851**

I was elated. Dr. Fine told me that our work had progressed to the point where I was ready to go off on my own. I was to complete a series of assignments in a book called *My Success Journal.* The results of these diary-like entries would reveal to Dr. Fine how far I had come and how much headway he had made in the finding and curing of CEO Dad syndrome. This was, Dr. Fine emphasized, a major turning point.

Up to now, my activities had been monitored or supervised. Here was an opportunity for me to take the initiative, to show off my new skill set, to demonstrate what Tom Stern could bring to the table. I was giddy. I felt like a little boy being asked to go to town with safety scissors, paste, and construction paper. What important thing would I make from my humble resources? Maybe the Roman Colosseum! Or a full-scale replica of the New York Stock Exchange! Or, maybe I'd just spend the afternoon eating the paste.

Remember, what you are about to read was written by a man who believed for all the world that he was forging ahead into new territory. When Dr. Fine gave me these assignments, he said, "There are no wrong answers."

Well, we'll see about that.

SUCCESS JOURNAL OF TOM STERN

SUNDAY. Create a six-point family mission statement. Get together with your loved ones and create a plan for living each day that is inclusive of the needs of the collective family unit.

What a treat it was to sit down with the people closest to me and draft an outline for living. I feel we did an excellent job deciding how their needs can be met within the parameters I set forth. Wow, evolving emotionally is so rewarding! Here's what we came up with.

1. Begin each day with Lou Dobbs or equivalent. Result: Agreed on in final vote of one for, three abstained.

2. Follow up with engaging daily appraisal of capital gains tax and how its effects ripple outward to touch everyone in the family. Result: Agreed on in final vote of one for, three left the room.

3. Tom will drop kids off at school three days a week. Let the record show that this was Chloe's suggestion and that Tom thanked her for being involved. The motion passed with the proviso that Tom will begin drop-off duties as soon as he gets a new car in which he can feel comfortable being seen while dropping off the kids. Points to Tom for growing as a person!

4. We will do more activities together as a family. Unanimous agreement. Tom added a corollary wherein he gets to decide whether to participate in each family activity based on his opinion of its worthiness and/or cost-effectiveness (e.g., he can refuse to shell out for that inane miniature golf course that is beneath the intellectual development of his children. I ask you, what do we gain as a family by spending three hours trying to tap a purple golf ball hard enough get it up over a hill and through a hole in the crotch of an eight-foot papier-mâché cowboy?).

5. Tom will make an effort to leave work at a reasonable hour in order to have more quality "alone" time with Chloe. Agreed unanimously, although Tom fought for and got the condition that when he cannot leave work, he will messenger money over in his absence.

6. Make a living will. For some reason, everyone agreed on this one pretty easily. And I'm not sure I like the way Chloe was eyeing me.

MONDAY. Good news! Madison Avenue has just given you one minute of airtime on national television, so that you can use this platform to let your family know how much you truly love them. Write the copy for your commercial.

Hey, gang! Do you have any idea how much a minute of national airtime costs? Just remember who they saw fit to trust with that kind of money, next time you wonder whether or not your dad and/or husband is the absolute bomb! Hey, how do you like the hotties in the skimpy outfits? They told me sex sells, and that it couldn't hurt to have the ladies to drive home the message for my ad campaign! And guess what? They wanted to relegate me to the late-night graveyard and a one-time-only run, but I negotiated. I played hardball with these bozos, and now it's going to run in prime time all week! How do you like them apples? Just in case you need any further proof that I AM THE MANNNNNN!!!!!! Well, they're telling me my minute's up. What's that? Do I have anything else to say? Nope, can't think of anything! Tom Stern rules!

TUESDAY. Take your daughter to work day.

Hey, Dr. Fine, I know what you're up to here! You want to involve a member of my family in what I do each day at work, thereby demystifying the process and giving me less of a reason to separate the work and home aspects of my life. Great thinking, Doc, and wait 'til you hear how I handled it. I went the extra mile.

Once I sat Grace down at my desk, she looked so natural there that I decided to let her start doing my job (with my guiding hand, of course!). You should have seen her conducting employee reviews. You haven't lived until you've heard a nine-year-old say, "Your performance has been, quite frankly, sub-par, and the sooner you clean out your desk, the sooner we can stop the bleeding."

Trust me, it was worth it to see the look on the face of the (now, former) office manager that day! (He didn't see me under the desk, giving cues to Grace, Cyrano-style.) And what a hoot when the gourmet food place delivered, and this little girl started going, "What's this supposed to be? I specifically said NO CILANTRO!"

She is certainly a chip off the old block. To think, Doc, I might have lived my entire life never seeing my daughter in her work environment, tearing out her hair and saying, "I am NOT precocious. These people are imbeciles!" And now, thanks to this Success Journal, I've already experienced it. Although I did have to upbraid her about one thing. At quarter to five, she impulsively buzzed the receptionist and told her to give everyone the rest of the day off.

The day off? Hey, I told her, if I don't get to have a life outside my job, why should they?

The day ended on a warm father-daughter bonding note, as we both stayed late at the office, which meant two dinners went cold at home that night. Better sign off. I'm starting to cry.

WEDNESDAY. Sit in on your son's school day.

Here again, Doc, I see what you're getting at. The more I normalize my family's activities outside the workplace, the closer we will become. See? I'm really coming along! Again, good thinking on your part, and I'm happy to report that, as hard as it was for me to take some time off the job, I really had a great time sitting in on J. D.'s fifth-grade language arts lesson today. It was like you had given my inner child permission to have a field day! Why, when J. D. misused the possessive form when he wrote the plural of "apple," my hand shot right up. "Mrs. Winslow!" I called out. "J. D. put an apostrophe there. But you don't use an apostrophe to indicate a plural."

Hearing a fifth-grade teacher say, "That's right, Thomas," was so empowering. It meant so much, I barely noticed J. D. slipping the class bully ten bucks or the bully saying, "I know where the old man's bus stop is. It's taken care of."

Then there's J. D.'s classmate Brian Skelton, whom I can't stand because his father once undercut me on this really big leveraged buyout. It was so much fun shooting spitballs at the back of that little brat's neck! I acted like I didn't know what he was talking about when he raised his hand and said, "Mrs. Winslow! J. D.'s dad is shooting spitballs at me!"

Mrs. Winslow took a sharp tone with me. "Mr. Stern," she asked, "were you shooting spitballs at Brian?"

"Yes, Mrs. Winslow," I answered. "One for each ten grand I'm going to donate to this school to help pay your salary. If you want, I can stop."

She looked shocked to think that someone her own age would resort to such childish tactics. Of course, after doing some quick math, she realized that a new car was only a few spitballs away and handed me another piece of paper. But, thanks to you, Dr. Fine, I was able to explore that side of myself.

The best part was there was a surprise quiz that day, and of course I finished it in five minutes and walked it up to the front of the class so everyone could see how much smarter I was than any of them. Little Susie Miller stuck her tongue out at me. But I don't care because I happen to know her father went bankrupt last year after he took a bogus stock tip from some junk bond trader and had to move the whole family out of the gated community.

Afterward, I thanked J. D. for the opportunity to see what his young life was really like. He said he had something important to do at recess and took off running, looking as anxious to get to his youthful day of fun as I've ever seen him. I've never been prouder.

Failing at Success

THURSDAY. Have a "date night" with your wife.

This was the best ever. We were a little late getting to the restaurant because I had to haggle with the babysitter. It had been so long since we'd had to hire a babysitter, and I felt it was outrageous for a person barely out of her teens to be asking for ten dollars for a few hours' work. Besides, as I informed her, haggling with me would give her invaluable negotiating experience for when she enters the job market. Who knows, thanks to me she might be able to bargain her boss at Orange Julius up to six bucks an hour.

Anyway, my date night with Chloe really brought back what things were like in the early days. It was so romantic when we circled the block eleven times looking for a parking space. Chloe fondly remembered that I object to paying for the valet, just on principle. We had a good laugh about how success hasn't changed me at all!

I had arranged for candlelight and for a violin player to drop by the table. There was some tense silence during which the violinist stood waiting for his tip, until Chloe finally reached into her evening bag and gave him five dollars. I explained to Chloe that I found the tension invigorating, that people in the violinist's position should not simply expect a gratuity. Needless to say, my wife left the waitress a tip in cash.

Afterward, we actually took the time to go to a movie, and Chloe valiantly stayed in her seat as fellow moviegoers hurled popcorn in my direction. I was moved by my wife's silent camaraderie during my numerous business calls. She was also very good at dodging the popcorn.

Finally, we stopped by Inspiration Point, that old make-out spot of our youth. I wrapped her in my arms and told her she was, without a doubt, one of my better investments. When she asked me what I meant, I told her that she was low-risk, she maintained a good rate of interest, and it would be years before she would depreciate.

She sighed and said, "With resentments compounded monthly." Later, as we got into bed, I asked her if she was in the mood for a merger. She replied, "Only if we can go to Neiman Marcus and make an acquisition." At that point, I declared Chapter 11, and we both went to sleep.

What a night. I feel alive again!

FRIDAY-SUNDAY. Start your weekend early and book two nights at a monastery. Allow time for quiet meditation and be ready to open to new awareness.

I have to hand it to you, Dr. Fine. This Success Journal is blowing my mind. That Zen retreat was the most incredible experience I've ever had!

First, I was supposed to sit quietly and concentrate only on the sounds of the chirping birds and the running water. Well, darned if all that quiet didn't get my mind buzzing right away! I stared long and hard at that stream of bubbling H2O, and I had a vision! This stuff was crisp, clear spring water, straight from the high-altitude thaw, and here it was going to waste as background music for some dopey meditation or contemplation or whatever. These monks were sitting on a gold mine! Bottle that stuff, cut a deal with a plastic manufacturer on the containers, and you could end up with an end per-unit cost of under ten cents, sell it for $1.59 a bottle, and then sit back and watch the cash roll in. Now, that's nirvana.

I immediately uncrossed my legs from the lotus position and went to find someone in charge. I located one of the junior exec monks, Master Liu, who was three months into a two-year vow of silence. Like that's going to hold me back when I've sunk my teeth into an idea as hot as this one!

"Hey, Master Liu!" I called out as I approached the little grotto in which he was sitting. "You gotta hear me out on this!" I began to give him the pitch on what I was now calling "Meditation Water." And I'll tell you, I have not lost my ability to work a room, or a grotto for that matter. Because strike me dead if old Master Liu didn't say, "Hmm. You may have something there." After which he slapped both hands across his mouth and his eyes went wide. He looked mortified.

"What's the matter?" I asked. "So you broke some silly vow of silence. We're talking long-term income here." Then I quipped, "Hey, I guess money does talk!"

He was slow in coming around, but eventually Master Liu had to bow down to— you guessed it—Master Tom. We started in on our five-point plan to convert the monastery into a manufac-turing plant. Liu roused all the monks from their meditations and offered them ground-floor opportunities as supervisors in the new facility. Believe me, those aesthetes jumped at the chance to give up sitting for eighteen hours a day, eating brown rice, and listening to a gong. A solid twelve bucks an hour turned their heads in no time.

There was a bit of a fuss when the regional overseer of this order of monks got wind of our plans. He said it went against everything a life of devotion to the Buddha and the eventual achieving of nirvana stood for. But, we took a meeting and I put it in perspective for him: What's one of his monasteries against annual profits in excess of $8 million, which he can use to buy all the brown rice he wants for his saffron-robed disciples? He came around, and now he even wants his picture on the bottle.

> To think all of this happened in one weekend. I don't know how to thank you, Doc, for opening up my life in so many ways with this Success Journal. Tomorrow, I will turn it in to you, and I just can't wait to hear what you have to say. I think I did pretty well, don't you? So, for now, "sayonara!"

I handed in the Success Journal to Dr. Fine that Monday, and by Thursday I still hadn't heard from him. I called his assistant, and she could only tell me that Dr. Fine had not been in all week. When I pressed her, she confided that when she tried to talk to him, he could not speak but simply kept bursting into uncontrollable sobs.

At first, I felt good. Obviously, Dr. Fine had finally realized his dream. He had found his CEO Dad patient zero, and now the latest evidence had shown him the road to a cure. He was beside himself, weeping tears of joy.

However, after another week went by I began to suspect that I was wrong in my assessment. Finally, one morning as I drove to work I spotted Dr. Fine walking down the street. I pulled up to the curb. Dr. Fine didn't seem to notice me at first or even that a car had entered his field of vision. He was wearing his lab coat and looked as if he hadn't eaten or bathed for days. He was wandering around like some sort of dazed pilgrim who had reached the end of his journey only to be confronted with a place whose very meaning he could not grasp. Or, to put it another way, he looked like Howard Hughes, distraught after just finding out he had lost his entire toenail collection.

Failing at Success

I got out of the car. "Dr. Fine," I said as I approached him.

First, he gave a start. Then, seeing that it was me, he relaxed. "Tom Stern," he said flatly.

"Did you get my Success Journal?"

"Oh, yes, yes, I got it." His shoulders drooped as if a thousand heavy winter coats had just been thrown onto his back. "Please go away, Tom. I can do nothing for you."

"But my Success Journal," I protested. "I was so proud of it."

Then Dr. Fine straightened up, and a strange brightness appeared in his now wide eyes. "Proud of it?" he squeaked. "You set my research back a hundred years. You taught your daughter how to fire somebody. You converted an entire monastery of Buddhists to capitalism. You are the most incorrigible, incurable CEO Dad I could ever have discovered. I cannot help you. Our work is finished!"

Dr. Fine turned and walked away.

I was stunned, but my old behaviors kicked in when I realized that Dr. Fine had just told me I had failed. In the world of the CEO Dad, failure is not an option.

"Oh, yeah?" I called after him. "Well, nobody tells Tom Stern that the work is finished! The work is finished when I say it's finished! I don't need you! I don't need anybody! I'll find the solution! You just watch!"

With that, I cut Dr. Fine out of my life. Okay, so he had pretty much cut me out of his life first, but, hey, I'm a CEO Dad, and I cannot give the impression of having backed down. I'm sure you understand. In any case, I was back to square one.

What is square one, anyway? A checkers term? Perhaps chess? These are the kinds of things I could have my editor look into.

I heard from her, by the way. It took a while for word to reach me, as the messages were in bottles that washed up on shore about eighty miles from my house. I'm forever indebted to the surfer who found the bottles and drove them to my home. I'm starting him in the mail room. Although my editor's messages arrived simultaneously, one was written earlier and the other one was an edited version, sent after she clearly had thought better of sending me a first draft. Here they are, side by side.

Dear Tom,

I don't know what island this is, but it's peaceful and I have found I can live on coconuts and the meat of great-crested thrushes. Civilization is a fool's game, a waste of time. There is no such thing as success! Everything is fleeting! Oh, and by the way, did I tell you my husband ran off with our nanny? The point is, I'm staying here for the rest of my life! I'm never coming back! Finish your stupid book without me! I'm telling you, I have seen the light! I am never, ever returning to the ridiculous rat race! Good riddance!

Kind regards,
Nora (use my real name, I don't care!)

Dear Tom,

Buried. Talk to you soon.

Your editor.

P.S. Did we ever settle that lawsuit about using my real name?
P.P.S. Ignore any previous drafts.

Sometimes I have to wonder if the journey I'm taking with this book is having an effect on my editor. What do you think?

★ ★ ★ Top Three Takeaways ★ ★ ★

1. **In our eagerness to change, we sometimes hope that every-thing can be made right overnight.** But modifying our behavior can take years. Not exactly what you want to read in a quick-fix, work-life balance, self-help book, is it?

2. **It is all too easy to turn projects that are meant to be inclusive of everyone into things that are "all about you."** However, in realizing this, you are, once again, making it all about you.

3. **A meditation practice can be quite helpful in calming the stress of daily life and getting you to rearrange your priorities.** Just don't come crying to me when you realize how damn boring it is.

8

Searching for the Big Idea

There's Nothing Like a Good Hostage Takeover

> "Education is a progressive discovery of our own ignorance." —**Will Durant**

> "You're fired, smart guy." —**Will Durant's boss**

Many years ago, when I was quite young and coping as best I could with being an underachieving drain on society, still blissfully unaware of the fulfillment that awaited me in using power, achievement, and work to block out all the meaningful things in my life, I was in love with a girl. We'll call her "Pam." Pam filled my heart with joy, gave a sense of purpose to my life. And I told her so, all the time.

One day, she broke up with me. Devastated, I asked her why. She told me I cared too much for her, that it made her nervous. She also mentioned a mole on my back that stimulated her gag reflex, but she assured me that was not the reason she wanted to call it quits, since with a little creativity she could avoid looking at my back for weeks at a time.

I couldn't understand what she was communicating to me. She was dumping me because I was devoted to her? Years later, I realized that Pam, conditioned by her upbringing to have diminished expectations, couldn't deal with the fact that she was being offered something real, something that could actually be good for her.

Pam ran away from my love rather than admit that she deserved better than what she was used to, and that I was willing to supply it. I'm certain that's what was going on because she took great pains to emphasize that her departure had nothing to do with my leaving toothpaste spray on the mirror after I brush. This was, she said, a small point, and so I have to conclude that the break-up was brought on by her fear of welcoming positive change into her life.

Now, twenty-five years later, I see that, in my own way, I was behaving like Pam. Thankfully, it did not involve secret sojourns to the women's lingerie department or an urge to lip-synch Barbra Streisand.

No, the way I behaved like my old girlfriend is that I forced Dr. Fine out of my life with my persistent unconscious behavior.

He was extending a much-needed hand, and I pushed him away because somewhere inside I felt I didn't deserve it. This all came to me much later.

What stayed with me after the good doctor walked away was that I was angry. I had failed at something I had set out to conquer, and it was driving me crazy. In fact, as I was about to find out, my personal train was hurtling headlong into nutball station, and all it would take was a little nudge to send me crashing into the stressed-out, achievement-mad depot of the insane. Ironically, it was Dr. Fine who gave me that nudge, although he couldn't have known what he would set in motion.

One morning I opened my door to find a Barneys New York bag on the front porch. Inside were a stack of books and a note from Dr. Fine.

Dear Tom,

I regret that I have been unable to guide you to sanity. Perhaps you will find some inspiration in these tomes, which were written by respected colleagues of mine. They have provided direction and inspiration for others, and perhaps they will for you, as well.

P.S. I've changed my cell phone number. And my locks.

Fine, Dr. Fine, I thought. Let's see what these pundits have to say.

I began with *Who Needs Extra Blankets When You've Got Inner Warmth?* by Ezekiel K. Lungeworthy, Ph.D. Dr. Lungeworthy saw life as a river.

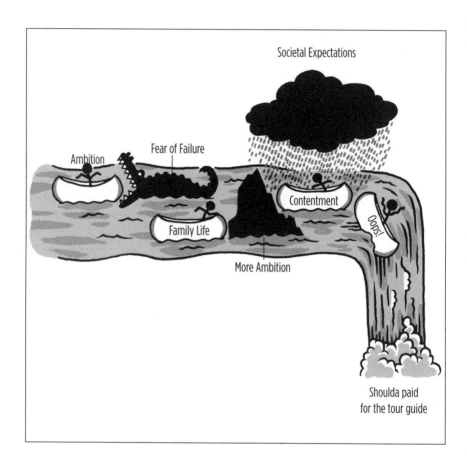

But that book didn't speak to me. I tried another of Dr. Fine's recommendations: *You Can Have It All! (Except You Can't, You Moron!)* by August Drane and Roberta Upshot. Drane and Upshot saw life as a tree.

Again, I was unclear as to what the authors were trying to get across. So, I picked up *Empowerment, Empowerment, Empowerment: The Three Most Important Things in the Real Estate of Your Life* by Dr. Bethany Roughy. Dr. Roughy saw life as a mountain.

Well, that does it, I thought. These people have nothing to teach me! I don't know what Dr. Fine thought I would get out of these books, but they succeeded only in fueling my fight-or-flight impulse. And believe me, flight was fighting fight, and fight was losing the fight to flight. Take that, editor!

At the point when I could have embraced the new, I resisted. I rejected the chance to grow. I did not see my earlier sessions with Dr. Fine, the attempts to integrate my progress into the workplace, or the data collected by Winnick, Warwick, and Wise as opportunities. I saw them as obstacles.

So what if my deep-seated need to win at all costs had resulted in an innocent researcher swallowing a tennis racket? So what if my family needed only the slightest provocation to point out what a weenie I was? These random facts didn't prove anything! In fact, they only showed that other people didn't get it. No one understood what it took to be a CEO Dad. CEO Dad syndrome was not an affliction, it was a birthright!

My regression continued, evidenced first in small ways.

One afternoon at the health club, I saw a man in a crowded sauna with a cell phone pressed to his ear. Brazenly, not caring who heard him or noticed the incongruity, he barked, "I'll have to call you back. I'm in a meeting."

This was my kind of guy! Nearly naked, and still pretending he was working. Talk about casual Friday! With people like this out there, why was I wasting my time with the likes of Dr. Fine?

A few weeks later, I sat in bumper-to-bumper traffic listening to some relaxation CDs. (My wife suckered me into buying them while we sat through a mind-numbingly dull PBS pledge drive. Honestly, as much as I live for the sound of seagulls and wind chimes, I could relax so much better if the CDs had the sounds of traders screaming on the stock exchange floor.)

Suddenly, a top-of-the-line Acura Legend coupe zoomed by in the carpool lane. I couldn't help noticing that the driver was alone in the car. He looked exhilarated and in his element behind his wraparound shades as he brazenly broke the traffic laws. And his license plate? "EATDUST."

Now there was someone who was grabbing life by the horns! There was a role model! There was what I had been missing during these past few months of ridiculous self-awareness training!

In retrospect, I probably shouldn't have gone out and bought all those Clint Eastwood DVDs. But boy, did they do the trick!

Clint doesn't take any guff from anybody! Shoot first, ask questions later! Do ya feel lucky? Go ahead, make my day! In fact, while you're at it, make my bed!

That's how you deal with those beneath your station! Let 'em stare down the barrel of a .44 Magnum, then see if they talk back! And Dirty Harry sure as heck doesn't need no "relationship" tying him down. What does he care if he gets home late? Does Harry Callahan feel obliged to help with the kids' homework? I think not!

Dr. Fine probably would have said that this kind of backlash was common, that I was in a difficult "hallway," and that the "right door" would soon reveal itself. He might have pointed out that it is exactly this kind of resistance to the process that produces the greatest breakthroughs.

But I no longer needed Dr. Fine to help me grow as a person! I certainly didn't need questionnaires, or diagrams, or Success

Journals, or volumes written by new age crazies who only scribbled their dumb books because they were losers who couldn't cut it in the real world. I didn't need anyone or anything! I would solve this problem the way I had solved every problem throughout my life—by myself, without assistance. And I would solve it in the place I always did: the workplace.

I suppose my staff expected a typical Monday meeting when I gathered them into my office. The more perceptive ones might have noticed the bags under my eyes and the fact that I hadn't shaved in a while. Or maybe even that I was wearing the same clothes I had worn on Friday. But no one would have noticed that I hadn't showered, because in the twenty-five years I've been in business, I have never let *anyone* get close enough to smell me.

When I paid the delivery person and stacked the thirty-five boxes of egg-and-cheese breakfast croissants on the coffee table, a few of my employees started looking worried.

When I locked the door behind the delivery person, several of the workers got dry mouth. I could see them swallowing hard.

Then, when I loosened my tie, they began to search each other's faces, hoping for escape or at least an explanation. But that wasn't going to happen.

"I'd like to thank you all for coming," I began. "We've had a good year. We've been productive. But now it's time to find out just how productive we can be."

I tossed a few buzzwords around: "Team players." "Bottom line." "Synergy."

Then I began the PowerPoint presentation I had stayed up all night preparing. It was an inspiring multimedia educational tool designed to help my people find their true power as individuals. I called it "Submit to My Will or Die." I'm surprised it took me so long to put it together since it was really just a series of graphics depicting me on a throne and the employees bowing at my feet.

Then I said, "Please, help yourselves to a breakfast croissant. These tasty egg-and-cheese delights will be our main source of nourishment for the next several weeks."

And then, leaning forward for emphasis, I looked around the room, making direct eye contact with every single employee, right down to the maintenance engineers, and said, "Nobody leaves this room until we come up with the big idea."

One brave soul, a woman I did not recognize, though she claims to have taken my dictation for the past eleven years, raised a timid hand and asked, "What big idea, sir?"

"I don't know," I answered. "I just don't know. But whatever it is, we're going to find it."

One staffer immediately panicked, leaping from his chair, screaming "Noooooo," and throwing himself against my corner-office window. He pounded on the glass pleading for help.

I ignored him. There would be no room for spineless suits in this meeting, and to acknowledge him would be to admit I needed an exit strategy. Oh, no, not me. Not the new Tom Stern, the one who had wasted his time on self-improvement for far too long. The one who had let some scientist try to tell him there was something wrong with him. Well, there was nothing wrong with me that a good steel spike driven into my skull couldn't fix!

I put up flowcharts, diagrams with arrows leading from "motivation" to "performance" to "profit" to "reputation" and back again.

I ordered a plaque online declaring me the Greatest Boss in the Free World, and had it shipped overnight. I made the driver set it outside the door, assuring him it was okay to leave it without a signature.

My employees could see him through the mottled glass of the office door, standing there in his shorts and filling out his computerized tracking form. One of them moved as if to shout for help, but she caught the crazed look in my eye and let her one hope of salvation walk away down the hall.

The days dragged on and on. I paced back and forth in front of my increasingly hungry and parched staffers. I needed no nutrition, no water, nothing. I was a force to be reckoned with. Employees were passing out at my feet. Finally, it came to me. The big idea. I shook my outstretched arms at the assembled group, some of whom had by now actually loosened their ties.

"Listen to me! I've got it! I know what we have to do! It's so simple!"

And then, I declared the solution to the world's problems, for all to hear: "WE MUST NEVER STOP WORKING!"

One brave young man stepped forward and offered his initial feedback on my groundbreaking new premise: "Are there any more croissants?"

"Don't you see?" I screamed. "If we never *stop* working, we'll never have to *start* doing anything else! There will be no other obligations—to parties, school functions, anniversary gifts, vacations—no, only work. Only sweet, blessed work, which never lets you down, never tells you you're inadequate. Work is the answer!"

I looked at the slack-jawed faces of the other people in the room. Why weren't they getting where I was coming from? It was time to appeal to their herd mentality.

"Join me! Leave your families! Leave your homes! Together, we will redefine productivity! We will set an example for the entire planet to follow! We'll have work retreats! Yes, yes, retreats where people go *just* to work. You must see the genius in that! Wait, wait, I have a name for our company: 'The Parent Corporation!' Oh, delicious irony!"

By this time, police and news choppers were circling outside the tenth-story window (perhaps you saw the coverage on CNBC?). On the street below, a negotiator called through a bullhorn, "Mr. Stern! I think it's safe to say you're a little stressed out!"

"Me? Not at all!" I shot back. I felt as clear as I'd ever felt about anything.

"We've got your family down here. They want to say a few words to you."

My wife took the bullhorn: "Honey, come home! I love you! You can watch all the ESPN you want, even those replays of the games from a hundred years ago! Honestly, I don't know what you see in them. I mean, you already know who wins and everything, plus they're on that grainy old film stock where you can't really see what's happening. By the way, who is Red Grange, anyway?"

Nice try, but not the most effective negotiation I'd come across. My family would have to do better than that if they were going to cut through my CEO Dad armor.

My son spoke next: "Dad! This is, uh. . . ." Unfortunately, the ADD kicked in before he could remember his name.

Finally, my youngest, Grace, called up from the street: "Daddy! The NASDAQ has been performing dismally ever since you've been gone!"

Bless the girl for playing it the way I taught her to play it, but the words had no effect. In fact, I had my assistant, what's-his-name, call Korn/Ferry and put them on retainer to begin a search for my new family.

"Forget it!" I cried. "I'm going to spend the rest of my life at work, and you can't stop me!"

Then, a strangely familiar voice rang out: "Tom! Get your sorry butt down here or you're fired!" It was the Chairman of the Board. "That means no expense account, no paid vacation, no company car, no 401(k), no health plan for dependents, nothing!"

I took a deep breath, weighing the options.

"Okay. Be right down," I said.

Just as suddenly as it had begun (actually, fifty-one hours and thirty-three minutes later), it was over.

I was arrested, tried, and released with three month's probation on a disturbing-the-peace charge.

My lawyer was able to claim extreme mental duress as a result of work pressures, and, as it turned out, the eighteen employees I kept holed up in my office decided not to press charges as long as they could be guaranteed that they would never have to work for me again. They settled instead for large out-of-court damages, and Korn/Ferry placed them all in rewarding new jobs.

My family, for reasons I still cannot pinpoint, decided to stick by me. It might have had something to do with the six-figure TV deal we were offered after my nationally televised breakdown.

It seemed we were a family America might want to see going about its daily business, and my wife and children apparently had no problem with inviting millions of viewers into our lives and our home on a weekly basis.

I guess they must have felt that after the dozen or so years of grief I had given them, they were entitled, at the very least, to their fifteen minutes of fame.

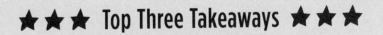

★ ★ ★ Top Three Takeaways ★ ★ ★

1. **No matter how thoroughly you may convince yourself to the contrary, you cannot handle every obstacle in your life by yourself.** Before you seek assistance from a human being, though, suck down some coffee and see if that helps.

2. **Our capacity for rejecting positive influences in our lives is in direct proportion to the capacity for acceptance of positive things we developed as children.** And our capacity for negative thinking is in direct proportion to how much we think about how little positive input we got as children. Raise your hand if you are confused.

3. **As for having a nervous breakdown and locking yourself in your office with a bunch of employees, well, don't try this at work.** 'Nuff said?

9

Playing with Fired

It's No Surprise When
I Get Canned on Camera

"If you can't get rid of the skeleton in your closet,
you'd best teach it to dance."
—Playwright George Bernard Shaw

"Sicko playwright caught dancing in closet with
skeleton!" **—National Enquirer**

They taped more than twenty episodes of *The Sterns,* but we
were canceled after the first one aired. The network told us
Americans just weren't ready to take such an unflinching look
at themselves, to confront their deep-seated materialism, to
see the extent to which they, as a nation, deprioritize emotional health. Pending copyright settlements, however, America will get another opportunity to use me and my family as a

barometer for all things dysfunctional when *The Sterns: The Complete First Season* arrives on DVD. Sadly, there will be no commentary track from yours truly. Things went a little south in the aftermarket contract negotiations. I believe the network's response was, "Have you considered radio ... preferably, CB radio?"

Before we go any further, let me just put this out there: If you, dear reader, are thinking of letting a television crew come into your home to record every waking moment in the lives of you and your family, go ahead. Who am I to stop you? But be ready to be chewed up, spit out, picked up and chewed some more, mashed into a fine pulp, swallowed, regurgitated and fed to the other hungry birdies, and finally sectioned and packaged in cello wrap, and sold by the pound at the meat counter of the human soul.

As a CEO Dad, I had been woefully out of touch with my own needs and those of my family. I had taken great pleasure in manipulating everyone in my business sphere until they came around to my way of thinking. I had ignored my employees' dissatisfaction and forged ahead without regard for even their minimum requirements. But at least I had never worked in TV.

In retrospect, I see my involvement with these subhuman life-forms as the straw that broke the CEO's back. I did not know it then, but my increasing befuddlement at the way I was being out-scumbagged at every turn was the beginning of my finally understanding who I was and how much I needed to change. But, as I said, I was not there yet.

Terence Flick was a big name in television, having directed live telecasts of *The Stupid People's Choice Awards* and *The*

World's Oldest Profession Pageant, as well as several episodes of the immensely popular drama series *Policemen, Doctors, and Lawyers: Special Unit Team Effect Squadron.* He was now following the money trail, branching out into reality television. With his straggly hair, messy beard, and ever-present flak vest, he hoped to give the impression that if he wasn't busy directing TV and living in a Bel Air mansion, he would definitely be covering insurgencies in developing countries.

I'll never forget my first meeting with him. "Hey, Ted!" he yelled out.

"It's Tom. Tom Stern."

"Right, Tom. Tom Burns."

"Tom Stern."

"Right. Anyway, Ted."

"Tom."

"Right. Tom. Listen, I really connected with you during that CNBC coverage. In fact, it was me that called in and gave them the dramatic tagline to use every time they came back from a commercial."

"Really? What was that again?"

"Deadly Deception: A Frightened CEO's Hostile Takeover."

"I don't think I was deadly. I never harmed anybody. And I don't see how 'deception' fits, either."

"Well, you're not in the business. You don't know what works. That's why the network hired me to tell your story."

"Well, that's true. I don't really know much about TV."

"See? There you go, Fred."

"Tom."

"Sorry, did I say 'Ted' again?"

"You said 'Fred' this time."

"Hey, apologies, there, Ted."

"Tom."

"Right."

At first, I took this show business superficiality in stride. I had made a lucrative deal with the network and knew that this was not my area of expertise. All too happily, I left the documenting of my life to the professionals. I could not have foreseen that I had essentially commissioned an outside entity to catch me, the wild CEO Dad, in my natural habitat with my guard down. A human nature documentary, if you will. If things went well, they might even get me lying in wait, then leaping from behind a desk to pounce on a copy of this year's disappointing annual report, ripping it to shreds with my teeth, and feeding the scraps to my children.

It's true what they say, that very soon you become inured to the presence of the video camera and the crew; very soon you simply begin behaving as you normally do, if for no other reason than to convince yourself that there isn't a small army following you around.

Each day, Terence would show highlights of the day's filming, and I would listen as he and his production staff howled with laughter at the antics of *The Sterns'* lead character: me.

Here are just a few of the scenes we viewed at the end of a typical day.

INTERIOR. STERN BEDROOM–NIGHT.
TOM and CHLOE sit up in bed, reading.

> *Chloe:* After all the work you did with Dr. Fine, would it kill you to show some kind of emotion?

Tom: Oh, I get it. I show some emotion, the strain kills me, and then you collect on the life insurance. Pretty slick.

Chloe: I'll take that as a "no."

The crew was rolling in the aisles after that one. I remember the sound guy going, "Where do you come up with this stuff?"

I was modest. I said I didn't even think about it; it just came out of me. The room went quiet after that. Well, of course, I thought, they are in awe of my natural ability to carry a scene on TV. I didn't realize that it had finally occurred to them exactly what kind of guy I was; in fact, they were terrified, and had frozen in place the same way one might when hoping not to get attacked by a mountain lion. ("Try to stay calm. . . . CEO Dads can smell fear."). But I had it in my mind that I was discovering gifts I didn't even know I had. Whole new vistas were opening up before my eyes! Just look at how I "killed" in the next snippet they cued up.

INTERIOR. TOM'S STUDY—NIGHT.
TOM sits across the desk from his son, J. D.

Tom: Grace is getting excellent grades. Why can't you, J. D.?

J.D.: I don't know, Dad. Maybe I need you to participate more in my life.

Tom: Please. Give me something I can work with.

The cameraman spit out his veggie wrap on that one. Look at the power I had to command the screen! These people were putty in my hands! I'd have their act down inside of a month, and then it would be look out, Hollywood! Of course, the cameras didn't just follow me around at home. They caught plenty of chuckles at work, too.

INTERIOR. TOM'S OFFICE–DAY.

TOM sits behind his desk. Across from him, WALTER, a nervous employee, paces back and forth while running a hand through his hair repeatedly.

> *Tom:* Look, Walter, I'm going to have to let you go.
> *Walter:* I knew it! Why?
> *Tom:* What do you mean, "Why?"
> *Walter:* I perform well, I'm punctual, I get along with everyone.
> *Tom:* That's all well and good, young man, but I'm afraid there's something here that's interfering with my basic sensibilities as a CEO.
> *Walter:* And what is that?
> *Tom:* Paying you.

The editing staff exchanged high-fives after that one. What most impressed the crew of *The Sterns,* though, was how I could, with ease and aplomb, regain control of even the most hostile home situation. This clip actually made it to the premiere (aka "final") episode of the show.

INTERIOR. STERN FAMILY DINING ROOM–NIGHT.

TOM sits at the head of the table, CHLOE to his right, J. D. and GRACE to his left. A SERVER adds a tureen of gravy to the sumptuous spread on the table, then EXITS.

Tom:	(Taps his fork against a glass.) Before we begin the meal, I think this is an excellent time for our six-month family review.
Chloe, J. D., *and Grace:*	Sigh.
Tom:	Overall, your performance has been strong, but some areas have room for improvement.
J. D.:	Fascist.
Chloe:	Nut job.
Grace:	Tyrant.
Tom:	Compliments will get you nowhere.

Now, that's what I'm talking about! It was me! That's right, me! I was bringing happiness to a group of strangers simply by being who I was! I was the linchpin in a complex operation designed to entertain and enlighten the entire country!

The idea that they might be laughing *at* me didn't even cross my mind. How could it? I was overjoyed. Here, at last, was the validation I had been seeking all my life. Here was an authority figure saying, "You're doing a good job."

Without realizing it, I had let Terence Flick stand in for my father and convinced myself that he was supplying me with everything I should have gotten from my dad. My twisted CEO Dad psyche began to see Terence as a gateway into mastering another high-maintenance arena, the imposing world of show business. By hanging around Terence, I thought, I could put yet-another notch in my successful businessman belt. Soon, there would be no area of corporate America in which I had not proved my innate superiority.

"Hey, Terence," I would call out across the bar during our post-shooting schmoozes. "Let's not end this relationship after we wrap production on *The Sterns*. I have some great ideas I think you and I could really get some heat behind."

"Oh, yeah, Fred?"

"Tom."

"Right. Tom Burns."

"Stern. Terence, the name of the show is *The Sterns*. I just said it two seconds ago. Why do you keep calling me Burns?"

"I'm sorry, Ted."

"Tom."

"Right. So anyway, Teddy my man, what are these ideas?"

I was so caught up in my quest to come out on top in the most high-profile, most prestigious business there is, that I began to find Terence's inability to remember who I was endearing. I told him about my idea for a look at the dog-eat-dog world of the trading floor called *Survivor: Wall Street*. I mentioned the concept of a show built around all the poor executives who lost their jobs to corruption, titled *Who Used to Be a Millionaire?* I shared my thoughts about a potentially powerful new drama involving a group of middle managers who become stranded on a desert island during an incentive-building retreat gone horribly wrong. All this chatter just to impress a man who was, I see now, out of my league in the most frightening sense. No matter how emotionally stunted I was, I would never reach Terence Flick's level of depravity. The man was unencumbered by even the slightest shred of empathy for anyone but himself. Was I envious? You bet!

As the weeks and months went by, as my personal life became fodder for the media, I got so caught up in the glitz and the glamour that I didn't notice how the emotional stakes were ramping up.

If I saw Terence standing a little too close to my wife, or heard her breaking into a self-conscious laugh at something he said, I blocked it out of my mind. That couldn't be Terence, going out of his way to let Chloe go ahead of him at the craft services table, could it? He never let anyone get ahead of him in anything, so why should he favor my wife at the buffet line? TV people are smooth in a way I could only dream of being. Sorry, in a way I *no longer* dream of being. (My editor made me put that in. This is a book about healing, after all.)

Oh, my editor? Yes, she's back. Long story. Here, I'm writing "editor update" on a Post-it right now. I promise I'll get to it by the end of the chapter.

Anyway, the machinery of television production is well oiled. If a network wants a hit, it will do everything in its power to make sure it gets one. The next time you hear the phrase *reality TV*, keep in mind that it won't make it to your screen until the director is happy with how that reality is going over with his focus groups.

Many a time we would hear Terence yell something like, "Cut! No, no, Chloe! When Tom goes to kiss you on the cheek, turn your head away! We need to get across the idea that he's physically repulsive to you or the whole concept of this show goes down the tubes!"

And then, when she got the take exactly the way Terence wanted it, he would rush over to give her a congratulatory hug, saying, "That's my girl!" Chloe fairly beamed with self-worth at the approbation.

Once Terence burst into a moment between Grace and me, shouting, "Grace, I don't see any reaction here! Your dad seems disappointed that you only got an A instead of an A-plus, and I need you to let me know how that feels! So, we're going again, and this time I want you to tear up that test in front of his face and kick him right in the shins!"

And she did. Terence said it made great television. To me it felt like great skin abrasions.

I didn't realize how Terence's little asides were nurturing the seeds of dissent in my family. Granted, those seeds were planted before our TV experience began, but if I had been smart and applied some of the knowledge I'd gained from my work with Dr. Fine, I might have been able to stop Terence from playing on my family's resentments. It turned out that Terence was following a script that would bring *The Sterns* to the dramatic conclusion the network demanded. And he had kept it a secret from me. But that final day of shooting is now etched in my memory. It took place in our family kitchen.

"Quiet on the set!" the assistant director called out.

"Ready, everyone?" asked Terence.

I entered the kitchen and poured myself a cup of coffee, my wife and children following.

Terence's voice behind me said, "All right, Chloe, kids? Remember what we talked about? And ... action!"

Chloe tapped me on the shoulder. I turned around, and there were my wife and kids, staring at me like a three-person jury.

"Tom," said Chloe, "we've talked about it and, well, ... you're fired."

The cameraman zoomed in for a close-up of my horrified face. "What?" I said, numbly.

"We're letting you go," Chloe continued. "It's just not working out."

"Come on," I protested. "That's the oldest line in the book."

"No, actually," Chloe said, "the oldest line in the book is 'Here's a gold watch.'"

At which point she handed me a gold watch. On the back was the engraved sentiment, "For ten years of excellent service. To yourself."

"You're just not fulfilling your promise as husband and father," Chloe told me.

"But I . . . ," I began to protest.

"Don't make this any harder than it already is," she said.

"Yeah, Dad," said Grace.

"What she said," said J. D.

My biggest childhood fear, that my father would let me go, had now come back to bite me. I was being fired by my family.

"This termination is effective immediately," Chloe said, stone-faced. "And we'd appreciate it if you would clean out your desk in a timely manner." Then she added, "I want you to know the door is always open to you, should you learn to modify your behavior on the job."

"Cut!" Terence screamed at Chloe. "We didn't talk about your adding that last bit!"

"Cut this!" Chloe shot back. "You got what you wanted, Terence."

Something was burning behind Terence's eyes as he glared at her.

Chloe had hit the wall. It was something to see. She folded her arms and said, "All right, we're done here. I want you and these cameras out of my house in exactly eight minutes, or I will involve the law."

Was it my imagination, or had my wife just channeled her inner CEO?

Before I could react, tell her how proud of her I was, she turned to me and said, "As for you, mister, this doesn't change anything. You're still fired."

In a last, desperate attempt at compromise, I smiled awkwardly and asked, "Are you sure you wouldn't consider a transfer?"

"OUT!"

As the crew packed up and a self-satisfied Terence Flick walked out of my house, I asked the sound guy if he could drive me to a hotel.

So, I had lost—truly lost—for the first time, and it was huge. Not only that, but I had lost to Terence Flick, a man more slick, ruthless, and uncaring than I could ever be. TV people proved to be corrupt in a way I was utterly unprepared for, but I had played my part in this tragic scenario, too. My deep-seated need for approval, my ongoing belief that every event presented a new foe to vanquish, had kept me from seeing that my inner jackass was being documented on videotape hour after hour, month after month.

I took a room in a fleabag motel. I felt lower than low, and the least I could do to honor that was not stay at a four-star establishment. I slept for days. At one point, I turned on the TV and heard some breaking entertainment news: Noted Hollywood mogul Terence Flick had signed a three-project deal with a major studio. Under the banner of his new production company, he would be overseeing *Survivor: Wall Street, Who Used to Be a Millionaire?*, and an as-yet-untitled project about a group of middle managers who become stranded on a desert island during an incentive-building retreat gone horribly wrong.

My first impulse was to call Terence at his office and tear him apart. Instead, for the first time, I took the opportunity to look at myself when something went wrong, to see what part I had played in my downfall. Sitting in a grimy room, fired by my wife and children, there was really no other place to look. So, when I did call Terence Flick's office, it was not to chew him out but to request a copy of every bit of videotape he had shot of me going about my business. It was time for me to take a good, hard look at myself. And there was nothing like two thousand hours of raw footage to give me that chance.

Oh, I promised an update on my editor. She turned up in Boise, Idaho, where a kind family by the name of Griswold took her in after finding her curled up on their doorstep. Following a few days of recuperation, she reportedly smiled at her hosts, thanked them for their hospitality, and walked to the nearest ATM. Two days later, she was back in her office in the city, clearing out her in-box and cutting deal after deal. No one has had the chutzpah to ask her what happened, and she acts as if nothing did. But I know what's really going on: she's in denial about a lot of her inner pain. At least I hope she is. That kind of stuff really sells books.

★ ★ ★ Top Three Takeaways ★ ★ ★

1. **Your need to succeed can convince you that you need to be better than everyone in every field of endeavor.** However, you are not an expert in everything. And I'm an expert on this subject, so I know.

2. **Television is a cruel miasma of dysfunction and empty promises, and trying to use it to validate your existence is foolhardy at best.** Of course, *your* life isn't a boxed DVD set about to ship at $29.95 a unit, is it? Just putting that out there.

3. **Sooner or later your family will no longer be able to function normally with a CEO Dad like you at the helm, and they will send out a cry for help.** You need to be open to hearing it and to acting accordingly. I recommend sobbing into your hotel pillow.

10

Drawing Out the Truth

When Life Gives You Lemons, Create a Comic Strip

"God is a comedian playing to an audience too afraid to laugh." **—Voltaire**

"Hello. Is this thing on?" **—God**

So there I was, holed up in the Scuzz Motel, chowing down chips from the vending machine, sitting cross-legged on a ragged twin bed, watching an endless stream of video images depicting me at my CEO Dad best (or worst, depending on how you look at it.) (Okay, yes, worst.)

As I viewed the unedited footage Terence and his crew had taped and examined my ongoing inexcusable behavior, I felt, for the first time in my life, embarrassed to be me. Watching myself alienate employees, potential clients, and my family, it finally hit—and I use the next word fully aware of its irony—*home*.

But the words my wife had spoken just before the final shot of *The Sterns* played over and over in my head and gave me hope. I had been fired by my family, sure, but Chloe had left the door open. She had said that if I came to my senses, I could come back.

This possibility boiled in my brainpan, and I started to do positive visualizations of what it would be like to return home. Once I got past the image of me ducking as pieces of hundred-year-old china hurtled past my head, I allowed myself to think about walking back through that doorway into a changed family dynamic.

Ironically, almost beautifully, it was my CEO Dad instincts, which had kept me going all my life and had just backfired so horribly, that pointed me toward a new business strategy. My gut told me that the answer was in these videotapes of me interacting with my loved ones and co-workers. The key to my survival, and to my rehabilitation, lay in that footage. And so I took it in, day after day after day.

A man on a mission, the significance of which I did not yet grasp, I arranged a leave of absence from my job. It was an odd feeling having my assistant put me through to my own voice mail. Not to mention having her ask, "What is this regarding?" when I called. Ashamed of who I was, I withdrew into a world of my own.

But wait. That was it! *A world of my own.* Gradually, the thought took shape: I needed to change my old world by inventing a new one. I needed to create an alternate universe in which the "me" that I used to be could be held up for scrutiny. I needed

... oh, yes, it was right there in front of me ... I needed to find the *humor* in what a poor role model I was! I would absorb the videotaped footage, take the raw and painful lessons it presented to me, and spin it into something I could laugh at. Something everyone could laugh at because they could see themselves in it.

Just thinking that made me feel better. If I could fashion something in which many people could see a bit of themselves, that meant that I was, as much as I had never wanted to face it, a lot like the rest of the people in the world. I wasn't—and no longer needed to push myself to be—superhuman. (Oh, boy. I think that was a genuine insight. It makes me feel so good inside, and nobody even paid me for it. Darn it, I'll just have to accept it: All introspection, no matter how transformative, is ultimately pro bono.)

Thus was born the comic strip *CEO DAD*—torn from the screen, as it were, but changed just enough so that I could poke fun at myself and be comfortable with the idea that I was being laughed at, not with. I figured it was the least I could do to give something back to the world.

From my base of operations at the Scuzz Motel, I began to bring my idea to fruition. In a fortuitous turn of events—one I took as a sign that I was on the right track—I discovered that Larry, the helpful concierge at the Scuzz, was a cartoonist. One day, as I reached across the counter for a fresh towel (which, at this place, meant it was only slightly crusty), I noticed his notepad, crammed full of doodles.

"Interesting," I said. "So you've created this whole combination of *Star Wars* and *Lord of the Rings*."

"Yeah," Larry said. "I just thought it would be cool if Obe Wan Kenobe had a bitchin' swordfight with Gandalf the Grey."

"Do you think you could draw a corporate executive and his family?"

"Do they live in outer space or Middle Earth?"

"No."

"Well, I'll give it a shot."

So, Larry and I gave it a shot. I paid him fairly for his work, which, in and of itself, was a breakthrough for me.

Gradually, we found a style and a presentation that clicked, and I began to sift through the events on the videotapes for comic-strip-worthy material. As you may have guessed, there was a vast and deep well of idiotic antics from which to, if you'll pardon the pun, draw. Such as this moment with my daughter, captured before I left for work one morning.

I should mention that I decided to name my comic strip family after where I had ended up in my life's journey, so in the illustrated version of my life we are called the "Pitts." The dad I named Frank, but I saw no reason to change the names of my wife and children. After all, they hadn't done anything wrong.

I would also like to mention that, having just come to an awareness of my comical attempts to climb ever higher on the corporate ladder, I enjoyed giving Frank Pitt the position of Styrofoam peanut packaging magnate. He was a man firmly stuck at the bottom of the middle section of the ladder, forever engaging in desperate behavior, always subconsciously trying to live up to the dreams proscribed for him by the dominant business paradigm of our culture—a paradigm that he not only doesn't question but embraces to a fault. Make no mistake, Frank Pitt is me. But if you're going to rip yourself a new one, I recommend using an assumed name.

All Larry and I had to do was watch all that footage from my reality show, and the strips virtually wrote themselves. Take, for example, the time I ran for Rules Committee Chairman of my gated community.

Drawing Out the Truth

Of course, I overcompensated for the loss by serving as campaign advisor on my son's run for class president.

Drawing Out the Truth

CEO ★ DAD

And let's not forget the workplace, where Frank Pitt got to deal with a harassment suit.

Drawing Out the Truth

Drawing Out the Truth

Throughout the process of bringing *CEO DAD* to life, I stopped by my old house often. The house in which my wife and family, who had terminated my employment, continued to dwell. So confident was I of being on the right track—so certain that making a cartoon of what a fool I'd been would be my ticket to marital reconciliation—that I made numerous visits to my family.

Well, actually I parked across the street. In the dark. Man, I was like a cop on a stakeout. A really wimpy, pathetic stakeout. I would gaze at my wife and children at their evening meal, lit by the dining room chandelier, their activity framed by the edges of the bay window. To me, they looked like the most wonderful painting there ever was. Though they did not know I was there, I drank in the sight of them as they smiled, shared highlights of their day with each other, and laughed derisively about what a jerk I was.

Okay, they didn't really do that last one. I know because I hired a lip reader to sit outside with me. Hey, I had to be sure. You'd do the same thing and you know it.

You may be wondering what they actually said. I can't remember exactly anymore, but it was mostly about schoolwork and how they liked the food. There was one passing comment about how the dog was enjoying my side of the bed, but I let it slide.

The truth is, they hardly talked about me at all. The old me would have fired the lip reader for being the messenger of truth, but the new me didn't. In fact, I gave him a referral—to a friend of mine who often found himself having lunch a few tables away from his main competitor. Thanks to information gleaned by my lip reader, my friend's competitor took a financial nosedive and can no longer afford to eat lunch anywhere. Funny how things work out.

The upshot of my clandestine visits to the homefront was that I shouldn't have expected my wife and kids to spend a lot of time discussing me. I had never made much of an effort to play a major role in their lives, so it wasn't like they were missing my presence.

But I'd show them. I was changing, and soon the whole world would know it. Or at least the people who read the funnies.

I spent ten, twelve, sometimes eighteen hours a day fashioning *CEO DAD* scenarios. This intensity felt different from the old days of being a workaholic. This was time spent in balancing the scales, putting things right. Months passed in the Scuzz Motel. Finally, I had cranked out a year's worth of strips. The final one was my love note to Chloe.

My fifty-two weeks of completed comic strips formed a dense tower, massive enough to take out several of the cockroaches in my room when dropped from a strategic height. My chest swelling with pride, I tucked the entire stack under my chin and carried it out to the car. I couldn't wait to show Chloe and tell her of my plans to get *CEO DAD* into every newspaper in the country.

With Larry's help, I had researched several of the nation's top syndicators, and I had made up my mind to go after the top banana, Harlan Samuels, owner of the Boffo Comics organization. And, for once, I wouldn't be reciting some diatribe about second-quarter returns or trying to twist the facts in order to close the deal. I would be speaking from my heart about something near and dear to me. Surely, Mr. Samuels would respond to such an outpouring.

I felt giddy. I wanted Chloe to be proud of me in a way I hadn't felt since we were first dating, back when we had had to beg and borrow to stretch every nickel, when we were head-over-heels for each other, when I didn't have gray nostril hairs starting to show.

The pile of comic strips teetering on the seat beside me, I pulled up in front of the house and parked behind an unfamiliar vehicle. I got out of my car, bending like a pretzel to balance the stack of *CEO DAD* strips, which I was about to walk over to show my beloved wife. As it turned out, my face was hidden behind the high-reaching mound of bristol board, so Chloe didn't see me when she stepped outside the front door to hug her departing visitor, the owner of the unfamiliar vehicle.

It was Terence Flick.

I stayed hidden behind my pet project as Chloe went back in the house and Terence drove away. Then, crushed, no longer caring about keeping the comic strips in order, I hurled them into the backseat, letting them fall willy-nilly across the upholstery. On my way back to the Scuzz Motel, I screeched to a halt at a dismal, misbegotten alleyway and threw the entire collection of *CEO DAD* comics onto a mound of old newspapers and decaying garbage. (Dr. Fine would have said this was a Freudian gesture. I would have had to admit that he was right, before giving him a gesture of my own.)

I drove away, crestfallen. I don't even know what "crestfallen" means, but it sounded right somehow. Bottom line here is, I had hit bottom. Again.

★ ★ ★ Top Three Takeaways ★ ★ ★

1. **Tapping into your creativity is a great way to counteract old conditioning from the business world, an arena that doesn't value free-form self-expression.** Of course, if it did value free-form self-expression, then all the loopy nuts who think they're artists would screw up everything in no time.

2. **Changing your environment, e.g., moving into a fleabag motel and forsaking creature comforts, can pare things down to their essentials and allow you the time you need to take a serious look at your shortcomings.** Or, to put it another way, when you've got nothing, you've got nothing to lose. Or, to put it another way, there really are such things as bedbugs, and, man, do they bite.

3. **After you admit some difficult things about your personality and how they have caused a rift in your personal and work lives, you may sometimes feel hopeless and wonder if there will ever be a place for you in the working world again.** Somewhere in that depressing sentence is an opening for personal growth through pain, but darned if I can spot it.

11

Getting to Less

Recovery Rocks!

> "When you gaze long into the abyss, the abyss also gazes into you." —**Nietzsche**

> "What're you lookin' at?" —**The abyss**

I made a darn fine barista. If you are thinking about dropping out of your so-called "important" job, let me tell you, the Daily Grind coffee house chain is not a half-bad place to start. We're talking full health coverage for part-timers, people! Not to mention the stock options. (They call them "bean stocks." Isn't that darling?). Plus, you get to work among the happy chatter of today's young urban professionals, gabbing about the latest films, fashions, and fads. So far, I haven't had the heart to tell them that MySpace.com is owned by Rupert Murdoch. It would break their little nonconformist hearts. But, oh, the constant whooshing of the frothy cappuccino machine! The calling out of the names written on the sides of the cups! The heady clack-clack of lonely would-be screenwriters tapping the contents of their tortured ids into their laptops! That's the life for me, man!

Honestly, working at Daily Grind is quite a treat. I enjoy a level of interaction with the world that I never experienced as a cog in the corporate wheel, I find no competition or ego-based insecurities among my fellow employees, and I now know that the phrase *tall drip* is not an insult aimed at a six-foot dullard but the term for a large regular coffee. This is notable because hardly anybody orders a regular coffee at Daily Grind. In a world of mochas, double decaf caps, and grande lattes, who needs it?

So, my life has settled into a familiar, calming routine, living at the Scuzz Motel, working at Daily Grind, and beginning work on what has now become this book. It feels like just the kind of shaking up I need to get back on my feet again. I am starting over at the bottom, and somehow it feels right. Why, it almost makes me forget that I've lost everything that was most important to me.

At the end of my shift I am often confronted by my loneliness and regret over how badly I botched my attempt to integrate my work and personal lives. My co-workers, college students whose piercings routinely set off airport metal detectors, only remind me of how far off track I've gone. Dylan, Oleander, Connor, and Persephone are nice, and they drag me along to the movies and shows they like. When we went to a Green Day concert, everyone there had an earring. I was the only one with ear *plugs.*

It's been somewhat fun for me, but, at the end of the day, these young people's priorities are different from mine. Actually, they are the natural priorities of kids barely into their twenties. They want to make enough money to enjoy life and to figure everything out later.

How uncomplicated could we all make our lives if only we kept that sensible attitude into full-fledged adulthood? Where did I veer off course? When did I convince myself that I needed more? When did that dream of more become something that needed constant feeding, to the detriment of all other areas of my existence? And was I the only one who felt so helpless?

Judging from the guy who got a low-grade concussion by repeatedly banging his head against his BlackBerry, I don't think I was.

His name was Bob Z, and he came into Daily Grind every day. He would order a grande mocha and sit for hours consulting his handheld communication device, frantically punching in information, switching back and forth between engaging with the BlackBerry screen and whipping out his cell phone to follow up on whatever oh-so-pertinent message blipped across the liquid crystal display.

We all knew him as Bob "Z," because Bob is such a common name that we would often ask for a surname initial to scrawl on the cup to keep our Bobs separate and easily identified. To many of my younger, less-experienced, co-workers, he seemed a pretty average Daily Grind denizen. After all, their generation was used to handling everything through technology. I'll never forget that touching moment by the tray of nonfat cranberry muffins when Oleander said to Dylan, "If you love me so much, why don't you just propose?" To which Dylan replied, "I did. Didn't you get my text message?"

But I saw something different in Bob Z. Something I knew only too well. Bob Z thought that even one second of downtime could mean an important deal going south. He was certain that a never-ending connection to the wheels of industry was his only hope of staying on top of the game. He forsook every other aspect of his life in the quest for the next big conquest, the next payoff, the next killing.

Bob Z was a CEO Dad.

At first, I said nothing. Just walked by his table, watched him slurp down his mocha, twitch toward the BlackBerry, jerk toward the cell phone. Slurp, twitch, jerk. Slurp, twitch, jerk. He was like a cat, constantly zeroing in on a new distraction in his field of vision. I wanted so badly to help him, but I had been down my own slippery slope of well-intentioned healing regimens, so I kept my distance. All the while, a little voice kept telling me that Bob Z was crazy, that I should stay away.

Actually, the little voice was Persephone, my co-worker, who thought Bob Z was "creepy."

"He's not creepy," I told her. "He's just late in coming to the consciousness that is necessary before true growth can occur."

"Whatever," she said.

One day, Bob Z came in and ordered herbal tea. The news went from barista to barista, each one more shocked than the last, and none more shocked than I was. As Bob Z came to the counter to collect his cup of hot water and a tea bag, I took a shot at striking up a conversation.

"No coffee today?" I queried.

"Didn't seem like the right thing today," he said. "A tea called 'calm' is just what the doctor ordered."

I watched from the counter as Bob Z sat at his usual table by the window, sipping his tea and . . . doing nothing. He just sat there, staring out at the bustling street, occasionally turning his head to note the arrival of other Daily Grind patrons. No BlackBerry, no cell phone, not so much as a notepad. Something had changed. I grabbed a wet rag and made my way toward Bob Z, using the wiping down of an adjacent table as a pretext.

"Just taking it easy today, huh?" I tossed out.

"Yeah," he said, quietly. "Ya ever wonder why we're all here?"

"Well, I'm not sure," I said, jokingly, "but something tells me it's not to have a very good time!"

With that, Bob Z burst into tears. And I did what any normal man would do when confronted with one of his fellows, broken and vulnerable to the point of sobbing. I turned my back and got the hell away from him. Oh, I did toss down a napkin in case he wanted to blow his nose.

Weeks passed. Bob Z returned each day, back to his old routine of slurp, twitch, jerk. It was as if whatever had caused his earlier outburst had never happened.

Then, on what would turn out to be a most fateful day, Bob Z sat at his regular table, took out his BlackBerry, stared deeply into its display screen, and began smashing it against his forehead. This being a coffee shop, half the patrons thought it was performance art and began to clap. It wasn't until Bob's head dropped onto the table and he failed to stand up to take a bow that people realized something was wrong and went to fetch the nearest barista. Which was me. I clocked out and accompanied Bob Z to the emergency room.

Something must have been in the water that night because Bob Z was not the only business professional in distress. The ER was filled with people like him, each with his or her own strange ailment. One man had come in after his middle finger got stuck in the up position during a traffic altercation. A woman was raving that her Bluetooth earpiece was biting her. And one unfortunate fellow needed several stitches after trying to receive a fax through his ear.

I think Bob Z and I were subconsciously taking note of these maladies and realizing we were far from alone that night. Bubbling in our brains was a profound idea: The need for some kind of solution to the work-induced crazies was going unaddressed.

It turned out Bob Z was not badly hurt, and, as he sat up in bed with a bandage on his forehead, I asked him what had prompted his man vs. BlackBerry attack.

He told me about working for ten years for a company (it shall go unnamed here) that kept sweeping his deeper needs under the rug by using the salve of promoting him. Now, he was a CEO, and he hardly knew how it had happened.

"You might notice that the only person here in the ER with me is you—almost a complete stranger," he said.

It hadn't occurred to me, but after he mentioned it I could see there was an anomaly: an outwardly successful-looking fellow who had no one to support him in a dark hour.

"They threw me out a few weeks ago," he said. "That day I ordered the tea."

Take note, reader: If you are suddenly motivated to switch from coffee to herbal tea and you don't know why, it might be time to invest in marriage counseling. I know, I know, it's not how you want to spend your money; but, come on, have you learned nothing from this book so far?

"You mean," I asked, nearly breathless, "you were *fired by your family?*"

"Exactly," he said. "That is the perfect way to put it."

And that, it could be said, was the spark—the opening gun, if you will—of the inspiration that would result in the birth of CEO Dads Anonymous.

The fortuitous meeting of Bob Z and me has by now passed into legend, but it is a testimony to my progress in the program that I do not have my ego invested in being such a part of history. Just the opposite, in fact.

What I know now is that all my attempts to "cure" my CEO Dad syndrome came from the wrong place: I was trying to fix myself for myself. Creating the comic strip was an attempt to turn my experience into something I could process and understand. Even as I tried to gain balance in my life, I was still making everything about me! The most important step in my recovery occurred when I realized that working to be a better person was not just for me, but for what I could give back to others.

Which, of course, meant they would have to give something back to me, too.

What? Am I going to help people for fun? What rock did you crawl out from under, buddy?

Okay, I am going to have slips like that. You don't heal overnight, after all.

Like any good recovery program, ours needed a name, and a corresponding, easy-to-remember, acronym. We tried GUYS WHO HAVE BEEN FIRED BY THEIR FAMILY AND LOATHE THEMSELVES ONLY TO DISCOVER THAT THEY WANT TO CHANGE, but GWHBFBTFALTOTDTTWTC didn't have quite the ring we were after.

We liked the simplicity of CEO Dads Anonymous but soon realized it was not inclusive of women. This was to be expected since we hadn't been very inclusive of the women in our lives up to this point. (Pretty enlightened, huh? See, we figured something out there! Brownie points, please.) Not to mention, there are plenty of women who picked up this book because they recognized certain behaviors in their own life. As I said before, CEO Dad syndrome is not gender specific.

Thus, Bob Z came up with the simple and to-the-point CEO Dads & Moms Anonymous, which not only was more inclusive but made a pretty decent acronym, CDMA.

Once that was out of the way, we figured we'd better come up with twelve steps. Hardwired for cutting corners, I suggested three four-step programs, if only for manageability. Bob Z vetoed this but agreed that perhaps we should have a different number of steps, to differentiate ourselves from the other recovery programs out there, and to accentuate the idea that we were not in competition with them. We settled finally on a ten-and-a-half-step program.

Why a half-step, you ask? Listen, Bob Z and I knew who we would be dealing with as the CDMA program grew. People like us. People who would constantly be fighting the urge to avoid feelings, to grab for more power, to want everything yesterday. The half-step was created as a symbolic gesture to those of us who struggle with the notion that there are not enough hours in the day, and that we just don't have time to make things better. It's a kind of playful tweak on the skin of the CEO Dad and Mom. Think of it as someone saying, "What, you can't even give us a half a step, you overachieving nut?" All right, so it's a little guilt inducing. You go with what works.

The Ten-and-a-Half Steps of
CEO Dads & Moms Anonymous

1. We understood that our lives had become unworkable as they were. Oh, who are we kidding? We were jerks and everyone hated us.

2. We came to the realization that a great and powerful being controlled everything. And that it was not us. Yes, CEO Dad syndrome sufferer, there is something greater than you. Live with it.

3. Admitting that there is a power greater than us, we surrender to it. Hold on, you *have* understood that there is a power greater than you, right? Come on, people, that was the step before this!

4. We must take a careful and unflinching look at all the things that make us defective. And, yes, bribing your children to get them to love you is defective.

5. We must make a list of everybody we have ticked off with our behavior and get in touch with them to apologize. (Helpful hint: E-mail is great for this. You never have to talk to them, they never get your home number, and you can send a handy link to www.forgive-me.com.)

6. In our continuing quest to be less defective, we must allow others to call us on our crap. When an aberrant behavior is pointed out, we must admit to it, and admit we were . . .

7. . . . always right about everything. Nothing is ever our fault. There. We gave you one step to regress.

8. Anyway, as we were saying, when we screw up and offend somebody, we have to admit that we're . . . ARGH! Really, sorry, this is one of the hardest ones. So, when we mess up we have to . . . we have to . . .

9. Wehavetoadmitwewerewrong! There, I said it.

10. All we have to do each day is ask that all-seeing power (no, not the Dow Jones . . . cut it out!) to help us carry out what is best for us and those we love.

10$\frac{1}{2}$. Share with others what you have learned along this path. Or, to put it another way, once you're all better, wave it in everyone's face and force them to come to meetings. Just kidding.

Getting to Less

The first meeting was attended by just Bob Z and me. So was the second. And the third. I should give a shout-out to my old company, by the way, who allowed us to have our meetings in the boiler room. Someone said something about "Why let church basements have all the fun?" but I don't remember who it was. In any case, no one from my old job ever came. I guess they were still scared of me after the "incident." Perhaps when my book comes out, it will let them know I am no longer a threat to them. Well, that and all the Step 5 e-mails I've been sending out. It really is so much easier when you know you don't have to have a conversation. And that "forgive-me" Web link is just so helpful. Everything you need in an easy-to-use template:

Dear (name of person whose life you ruined),

　　When I (inconvenienced/yelled at/vowed to ruin) you, I was in the grip of my unfortunate condition, CEO Dad syndrome. I know I can never make up for the way I (ticked you off/ripped you off/caused you to lose your house), but by reaching out this way I hope to leave room for you to (let bygones be bygones/bury the hatchet/bury the hatchet in my head if that's really how you're feeling).

Sincerely,

　　(CEO Dad syndrome sufferer)

By the time of our fourth meeting, word of our efforts had begun to trickle out into the community. People from all walks of life began to show up as the path that Bob Z and I were forging deepened our understanding of how common our problems were.

In the painful admissions of our attendees, we found a common bond and the hope of redemption. There was the high-powered corporate head who went broke designing a new line of clocks with thirty hours in a day (he only wanted, he wept, to give people more time to work). There was the influential businesswoman who had arranged for her meals to be administered intravenously during staff meetings. There was even a young entrepreneur who had made a fortune with his own online trading company; he was working to pass legislation that would make it legal for him to marry his computer.

Some of these people were incredibly powerful figures in the business world, who, according to the tenets of our program, must remain anonymous. But, let me tell you, these meetings are great places to network.

It is a big no-no to blow someone's anonymity, but there are two people who came to our early meetings who have agreed to be mentioned here, in the hope of providing inspiration to the reader.

Dr. Morton Fine is one.

My editor is the other. As before, we'll get to her later.

Dr. Fine told about how his research and attempts to codify CEO Dad syndrome were themselves the products of his ego, his quest for more power and stature. Like the rest of us, he was drawn to the meetings after hitting rock bottom. His was a particularly poignant crash and burn. He had been spending days at a time away from home, working on a project in secret at his lab, which he kept under lock and key. After a week went by with no word from him, authorities broke into his research facility to find him crawling around in a giant, sawdust-covered maze behind a glass partition. Dr. Fine had constructed a controlled environment for himself, in which he ran and ran like one of his lab rats, hitting wall after wall and sniffing. It took him days to stop jutting out his front teeth.

All right, perhaps it was crass of me to laugh at the end of his story, but I apologized profusely and he seemed to accept it. However, I'm pretty sure I racked up another Step 5 e-mail because he's been cold to me lately. Through his work in CDMA, Dr. Fine was able to patch up things with his estranged wife and reunite with his family. Yes, Dr. Fine had made that leap. What was my problem?

I re-read Step 4. I must still be defective or I, too, would be back in the bosom of my family, wouldn't I? What was I doing wrong that was making them withhold bosom from me? I wanted bosom, I needed bosom, and, damn it, I was entitled to bosom! This was when Bob Z pulled a Step 6 (the "calling me on my crap" one), and I struggled with Steps 7, 8, and 9 (the admitting I was wr—well, you know what I mean). Bob pointed out that I was holding on to so many resentments regarding my family that I had become stuck.

I was doing all this work on myself, so why weren't my loved ones admiring that and welcoming me back home? Yet, had I really ever reached out to them? Hadn't I kept up only minimal contact out of my fear of change? How badly did I want to succeed at being a husband and father? How was I to gauge success in this nebulous arena? (How many more hypothetical questions can I pose in one paragraph?)

The emotional bottom line was that I couldn't measure my value to the wife and kids with a paycheck or a killer business deal. That's what got me fired in the first place!

Bob Z illuminated for me the need to just take the plunge. Still stinging from seeing Terence Flick with my wife, I told Bob that I didn't think I could do it. He suggested I start by reaching out to the kids.

May I say to you, my reader, that getting the proper balance in this reconciliation-with-loved-ones business is not easy. Case in point:

"Hello."

"Hi, J. D., this is your father."

"Oh. Hey, Dad."

"What's up?"

"Nothing."

"How's school?"

"Okay."

"Listen, J. D ... ?"

"Yeah?"

"Well, it's just, um, I see now that for years I was overcompensating for my lack of confidence, and acting not out of my own desires but out of those of my parents, and then projecting all that misdirected need onto you by allowing you to become someone who didn't measure up and thereby negating you as a person when really I was negating myself and was too burdened by inner shame and inadequacy to deal with that. You can see that, can't you, son? Hello? J. D.? Hello?"

Getting to Less

He had hung up. Okay, so it was too much, too soon.

The call to my daughter, Grace, found me taking a different tack.

"Hello."

"Hello, Grace, this is your father."

"Hi, Dad."

"How's everything?"

"Okay."

"How's school?"

"Good."

"Anyway, Grace, I'm just calling to let you know I care about you."

"That's good, Dad. But I get the feeling that for years you were overcompensating for your lack of confidence and acting not out of your own desires but out of those of your parents, and then projecting all that misdirected need onto me by allowing me to become someone who didn't measure up and thereby negating me as a person when really you were negating yourself and were too burdened by inner shame and inadequacy to deal with that. Hello? Dad? Hello?"

There was a time when hanging up on my daughter would have meant I had won. Those days, fortunately, were gone.

I knew I had to reach out to my wife next, or try to, but I was still wounded, unable to admit what I had done wrong in light of having seen her with Terence Flick.

Which brings me to my editor.

Before she dragged herself to a meeting, my editor thought she was okay. She had gone back to work as usual, seeking solace in the fast-paced milieu of publishing and its familiar dog-eat-dog dynamic. She did not know that undiagnosed CEO Dad syndrome, left to its own devices, is a progressive disease.

Her condition began to manifest itself in troubling ways. She began to edit. Everything. It started in small ways. Calling the *New York Times* to tell them their story on the transit strike could have been trimmed from 500 words to 463. Losing her temper at a business luncheon and screaming at an important client, "Just ask for the chicken! You don't have to order "Chicken a la Fromaggio Primavera! It's the only chicken dish on the whole freaking menu! Just say you want the chicken; it's a much more effective use of words!"

As her business suffered, the money stopped coming in and she began to survive on canned soup. Even then, she would mentally edit the product information on the soup can label. ("They already described the soup as 'delicious' in the opening sentence! It's superfluous to call it 'mouthwatering' only 26 words later!")

Finally, when she found herself on the highway screaming at the owner of the vanity plate in front of her—"Moms Taxi? Where's the apostrophe, moron?"—she knew it was time for CDMA.

Over the course of several meetings, she shared about how she had been unhappy in her marriage for years and was using work to avoid confronting her husband. When her husband began to stray, she blamed him without looking at how she had withdrawn from the marriage and without communicating her dissatisfaction. She would never have known to seek help, she said, if it weren't for the CDMA flyers Bob Z and I had plastered all over the scaffolding and telephone poles in the area. (This, incidentally, led to an ongoing flyer-plastering war with a local heavy metal band called "The Running Sores," but that's another story.)

Now, my editor said, she was doing much better. She was clocking out of work at exactly five each day, she was taking time to walk the dog and make herself healthy meals, and she had just begun a satisfying relationship with a man she described as the most exciting, wonderful guy she had ever met. His name was Terence Flick.

My heart skipped a beat.

Part of me wanted to warn her against going anywhere near this toxic slug, but mostly I was thinking that if she was with Terence, then Chloe probably was not. Sure, there was a chance that Terence, ever the slime mold, could be two-timing her, but I simply had to believe otherwise. I had to believe that Chloe was through with the bum and that I could finally step in as her rightful guy.

In hindsight, I suppose I should have warned my editor about how manipulative and repugnant Terence Flick was. But, hey, people have to make their own mistakes, right? It's one of the rules of the program. It's not in the main $10\frac{1}{2}$ steps. It's a subclause. Page 32, paragraph 8. Really, you can look it up.

Emboldened by my certainty that Chloe had passed through her phase of lashing out at me through another man, I drove toward my home, my true home, the home that I now wanted more than anything I had ever wanted in my life. More than any corner office, or company car, or expense-account lunch, or out-of-town seminar.

I had written a heartfelt poem to accompany my return, hoping Chloe would remember that I had not written her a poem since we were first dating. I still remember that one, written by a more naive me, almost twenty-five years ago:

> *Roses are red*
> *Violets are blue*
> *I'm pretty sure you love me*
> *So I guess I'll love you, too.*

I nearly swooned at the romance of it. But I wanted this new poem to say even more. And so it was that I wrote,

> *Roses are red*
> *I've been a fool*
> *Putting work over family*
> *Is simply not cool.*

Tom Stern, proud 10½-stepper and recent Daily Grind Barista of the Month, was going home. Provided home would have him.

★ ★ ★ Top Three Takeaways ★ ★ ★

1. **Working as a clerk at a food service retailer is an excellent way to get in touch with what is happening outside the confines of your soul-destroying job.** And did you know that The Daily Grind also sells CDs of eclectic and interesting music? (There, contractual obligation fulfilled.)

2. **No matter how low you have sunk in your inability to balance work and family, you can always find a sympathetic group of people who have been where you are.** However, if you don't help put away the chairs after a meeting, you will be scowled at.

3. **It is never too late to start over.** Okay, maybe not never. Say you're, like, 98 years old. It's probably okay to coast at that point.

OUTroduction

I got a little choked up the day I quit my job at Daily Grind. It was tough saying good-bye to the gang, and I was in a lot of pain. Mostly from the eyebrow-piercing they convinced me to get. They failed to tell me how incredibly close to the bone the skin on your eyebrow is and how long the puncture wound would itch. Still, it's a badge of honor, and I wear it proudly. Like the Shaolin monk who walks barefoot over hot coals to test his faith, I now bear a physical memento of my time getting back to what is real. My time of enlightenment.

True, a monk spends a lifetime immersing himself in one of the world's most ancient religions and endures many years of self-deprivation, and I spent six months in food service; but this is America, so it feels like about the same thing.

And, like one who devotes his or her life to seeking deeper knowledge, I am learning each day that true enlightenment may never come. In fact, as I write this, I have just hurled my phone across the room in response to losing a client I thought was in the bag. The difference now is that I get up from my desk, walk calmly across the room, and apologize to the phone. Yes, it's an inanimate object, but, believe me, if you can beg a telephone for forgiveness, beseeching your wife is a cakewalk.

I got this pearl of wisdom from Dr. Morton Fine, who continues to work the 10½ steps of CDMA with Bob Z and me, and has established a new research institute called the *I'm Only Here to Nudge You in the Right Direction* clinic. He has found that there is power in words and that this new clinical direction helps remove his ego from the process. He works much more effectively now, and his success rate is phenomenal. If your boss has inexplicably hugged you recently, that's probably Dr. Fine's doing. If your boss has taken a six-week leave of absence to become certified as a massage therapist in order to give the entire staff rubdowns during lunch, that is *definitely* Dr. Fine's doing.

My editor is still a fixture at CDMA meetings. She stopped coming for a while during the height of her romantic involvement with Terence Flick, secretly guilty about allowing herself to be seduced by the allure of his untreated CEO Dad syndrome. What follows is, in her own words, what happened.

He was so ambitious, so ready to take on the world. I found him sexy and dynamic. I didn't see that I was attracted to the same qualities I used to have and that I was living vicariously through him, postponing my healing. I didn't notice how he began to reinforce and even encourage my compulsion to edit everything.

I should have suspected something when he kept asking me how to rephrase what he wrote or said.

"You're so smart," he would say then, sweetly. "You really know your stuff. I have so much to learn from you."

OUTroduction

I thought nothing of it. It felt as if Terence was being respectful of my compulsions. It wasn't until I saw the script he carelessly left on the kitchen table one morning that I discovered the terrible truth. The front page read,

CUT IT OUT
A proposal for a reality series about people who can't stop editing everything.
By Terence Flick, all on his own, with no help from anybody.

It was then that I made the most important edit I have ever made, before or since. I cut Terence Flick out of my life.

My editor brought Terence to a meeting before she gave him the boot. I wasn't there, but Bob Z told me he said something like, "Wait a minute, you're telling me I'm responsible for my own behavior and the effect it has on others? You people are freaks!"

Don't expect the content of television programming to improve anytime soon.

Bob Z and I continue our work with CDMA, and we have both gone back to our old jobs. Bob took on his executive position with new vigor, realizing that it was the *second* most important thing in his life. The first being major league baseball. Kidding. The first being his family, of course.

I went back to recruiting corporate clients for my headhunting company, only now I'm kind and truthful during every step of the process. Dr. Fine assured me that breaking out in a cold sweat while being kind and truthful is completely normal, and that it will pass in as little as eight years.

Whenever I feel the urge to revert to my former high-maintenance ways, I give the eyebrow-piercing a little tug. It keeps me honest.

Plus, as perhaps a subconscious reminder about my priorities, I am now a telecommuter. I *work* out of my *home,* and the irony is not lost on me. When the kids forget it's business hours and walk in on an important call, I don't glare at them or wave at them to shoo. Far from it. I gesture toward the chair across from my desk, miming graciously how they may sit and watch their father work.

When the phone call is over, I invite Grace and J. D. to ask questions, involving them in those aspects of work that really are rewarding, that really do provide satisfaction in a job well done.

The effect has been tremendous. My children say, "Whatever," and then go off to download songs to their iPods. Believe me, this is progress.

The important thing is that they now have a general sense that I love them with all my heart, which is far preferable to the general sense that I *have* no heart. (It still hurts to remember Grace's third-grade science fair project, in which she sought to prove that ice water really did run through my veins. The diagrams were very convincing.)

Oh, and I only have to work part-time now, owing to the success of the *CEO DAD* comic strip, which got picked up for national syndication in major newspapers. It was all very simple, really.

OUTroduction

As you will recall, after seeing red when I watched my wife hug Terence Flick, I threw away the entire stack of completed strips. They were retrieved by a homeless man named Victor, who found their consistency ideal as a sleeping surface. Victor's home base was an alley around the corner from a prestigious opera company, and attending the local premiere of *Tosca* one evening was the aforementioned Harlan Samuels, lifelong opera fanatic and owner of Boffo, the multimillion-dollar cartoon syndicator.

As Samuels walked by with his wife, Belinda, Victor appealed to him for some spare change. Samuels, noted for his many contributions to the less fortunate, was only too happy to give Victor a twenty-dollar bill.

As Samuels crouched to press the bill into Victor's hand, his eyes fell on the panels of a comic strip under Victor's head. As comics were his business, Samuels asked Victor to move a little to the left, and proceeded to read several installments of *CEO DAD*.

He laughed, then showed them to his wife, who also laughed. (A very good thing. Word on the street is if Belinda doesn't laugh, the strip is dead in the water.)

Samuels tracked me down and offered me a very satisfactory one-year renewable contract, which I didn't even bother to negotiate.

So you see how, once you begin the oh-so-important but admittedly daunting task of self-improvement, things can line up in ways you never expected.

And don't think I don't know that I owe my success in the papers to a homeless man. Who, by the way, is no longer homeless. Let's just say Mr. and Mrs. Samuels were very impressed with the way he sang that aria from *La Traviata*. I believe he opens in Madrid on Tuesday.

I have worked with several illustrators since the early days of the *CEO DAD* strip. Larry moved on, going in a much darker direction with his own strip, *DICTATOR DAD*. It deals with the wacky adventures of a lovable Third World maniac who will stop at nothing to seize power from the entrenched bourgeois government. The only time he sees his three wives and nine children is when he needs them so he can drive in the carpool lane.

I was able to bring myself to read only a few installments. It was a little unsettling to see someone who looked like me sitting on a skull-laden throne, holding a machete and screaming at his wireless provider. Larry confessed that working with me gave him the idea for *DICTATOR DAD*. Further proof that my recovery is an ongoing thing.

Well, I guess that brings us up to date.

Oh, wait a second, my wife is calling me from the other room. I can't hear what she's saying.

Oh, she says she just wants me to know that she loves me.

I, of course, yell back that I love her, too. More and more each day. Sickening, isn't it?

She never was involved with Terence Flick. That was all a figment of my jealous, insecure imagination. I *wanted* her to be seeing that blowhard because it made it easier for me to shift some of the blame for my having been fired by my family.

I should have given Chloe more credit, but I guess I was worried. After all, she had fallen for me, and I was a shallow, manipulative greed-head. Maybe she wanted to upgrade to the luxury model.

In fact, Terence had come by that night to see if she was available, but what I witnessed was a thanks-but-no-thanks good-bye. Chloe knew I was parked in front of the house, and told me later that if I had only looked closely, I would have seen her making a gag-me face over Terence's shoulder.

Some months later, the day I raced over to the house with my love poem clutched in my shaking hand, Chloe invited me in. She thought the poem was awful, but it did the trick.

So, here it is, just about five o'clock on a Friday, and I'm about to put the phone on "do not disturb." I put my feet up. My heels balance precariously on the edge of the desk. You know, the heels of my shoes might well be scuffing the desktop. What if there were some sort of protective rubber stripping a person could put on his or her desk to prevent that kind of thing? Why, I'll bet executives across the country would eat that up as a novelty item! What to call it? "The Feeter-Upper?" "The Dog Catcher?" Never mind, I'll come up with a name later. The point is, I'd better get on this. Gotta stay ahead of the competition. I'll put in a call to a patent lawyer, then I'll get going on finding a manufacturer who can make me a prototype. It's not too early to start soliciting investors. I'll take the lion's share, of course, but I'll need some big capital to get this idea off the ground. I know— I'll call Bob Z. He knows that consultant who knows the other consultant who knows that designer. I have to find out what he would charge RIGHT NOW. This has to be taken care of RIGHT NOW. There's a lot of money at stake here, and time is of the—

Hold on, that's my wife again. Can't quite hear what she's saying.

It was, "I don't care what you're thinking about, you are not going near that phone. Whatever it is, it can wait."

It's uncanny how she does that. From two rooms away, even.

She's right, of course. And we do have plans as a family tonight. Dinner and a movie. Okay, so we're taking the kids out to save money on a sitter, but by the time you buy them both their tickets, popcorn, and candy, it works out to even more than a sitter, anyway.

Whoops, old behavior creeping in again. It takes work, people. I'm not here to tell you any different. But I know now that the truth will reveal itself sooner than it used to.

And the truth is, you can't put a price tag on quality time with your family. But, if you do, always mark it down around the holidays. Just kidding.

 **Top Three Takeaways**

1. **Come on, the book is over.** You still want takeaways?

2. **What is it with you and this insatiable appetite for information?** Have you learned nothing?

3. **All right, all right, you want a takeaway, I'll give you a take-away:** You steal my "Feeter-Upper" idea while I'm out having a good time with my family, and I will see you in court!